# FREEDOM TO BE

## Experiencing and Expressing Your Total Being

Everett Shostrom, Ph.D.

PRENTICE-HALL, INC.
*Englewood Cliffs, N.J.*

Illustrations adapted from copyrighted charts provided
through the courtesy of The Institute of Therapeutic Psychology,
Santa Ana, California.

*Freedom to Be: Experiencing and Expressing Your Total Being*
By Everett Shostrom, Ph.D.
Copyright © 1972 by Everett Shostrom, Ph.D.
Illustrations copyright © 1972 by Everett Shostrom, Ph.D.
All rights reserved. No part of this book may be
reproduced in any form or by any means, except
for the inclusion of brief quotations in a review,
without permission in writing from the publisher.
Printed in the United States of America
Prentice-Hall International, Inc., London
Prentice-Hall of Australia, Pty. Ltd., North Sydney
Prentice-Hall of Canada, Ltd., Toronto
Prentice-Hall of India Private Ltd., New Delhi
Prentice-Hall of Japan, Inc., Tokyo

**Library of Congress Cataloging in Publication Data**
Shostrom, Everett L
Freedom to be.
Bibliography: p.
I. Self-actualization. I. Title.
BF697.S54  131'.32  72-5332
ISBN 0-13-330621-6

10 9 8 7 6 5 4 3 2

*To The Magnificent Men*

BOOKS BY EVERETT L. SHOSTROM

*The Dynamics of the Counseling Process*
(with L. M. Brammer)

*With This Ring*
(with Judge Louis Burke)

*Th rapeutic Psychology, Fundamentals of Actualization
Counseling and Psychotherapy*
(with L. M. Brammer)

*Man, the Manipulator*

*The Manipulator and the Church*
(with M. Dunnam and G. Herbertson)

*Between Man and Woman*
(with J. Kavanaugh)

*Freedom to Be*

# Acknowledgments

I am grateful to the Magnificent Men of Chapter 10 who have become my models for actualization: Abraham Maslow, Gardner Murphy, Carl Rogers, Rollo May, Paul Tillich, Victor Frankl, Frederick Perls, and Alan Watts. Each of them has had a particular and unique influence on my work and life. I am indebted to Virginia Satir, a truly free being, for the encouragement and help in the classification of the manipulative response forms. The staff of the Institute of Therapeutic Psychology has been especially helpful in their contributions to the ideas that fill this volume. These include Robert Hilton, Alan Levy, Neil Matheson, William Pickering, Jacquie Pomeroy, and Mary Wells. My dear friend Mary Stuttle has again been valiant in her typing efforts.

I want to express special gratitude to George Bishop, an actualizing friend, for his assistance in the development and editing of this volume.

In my opinion, Richard M. Nixon has exemplified many of the growth processes expressed in this book through his rise to the presidency. I am indebted to him for serving as a public model for the theory of the book.

# Preface

A recent graduate from therapy put it this way:

I was having dinner with an old friend I had not seen for some time at a plush San Francisco restaurant. Having known me before as a typical businessman with a brash front of assertion and strength, she was shocked when I unashamedly began to cry, to feel my weakness, and express my tenderness openly to her. She exclaimed, "My God, you're different now, you're a *total* being!"

The goal of this volume is to help the reader experience and express his *total* being on the polarities of strength-weakness and anger-love. To achieve the goal of becoming total appears deceptively simple, but the achieving of it is a difficult though exciting and rewarding adventure.

Most of us, because of early experiences, have cut off one or more of the polarities in our attempts to experience and express ourselves. Whereas being self-actuali*zed* may be defined as the *total* expression of our unique beings, most of us are only *partial* in this ability to be fully ourselves. Hopefully, however, this book can help us to become more total in our expression, to become more and more self-actuali*zing*.

# CONTENTS

|  | INTRODUCTION | 8 |
|---|---|---|
| *Part One* | **THEORY** | |
| | 1 The Uncharted Course | 15 |
| | 2 Survival vs. Growth | 27 |
| | 3 Tertium Quid | 41 |
| | 4 From Actualization to Abnormality | 55 |
| *Part Two* | **APPLICATIONS TO THERAPEUTIC CHANGE** | |
| | 5 Expanding Emotional Expression | 65 |
| | 6 Bodily Expressions of Rhythm | 75 |
| | 7 Questioning Our Assumptions | 89 |
| *Part Three* | **APPLICATIONS TO LIFE, LOVE, AND MARRIAGE** | |
| | 8 Love, the Human Encounter | 103 |
| | 9 A Declaration of Marital Freedom | 113 |
| | 10 Magnificent Men | 123 |
| *Part Four* | **APPLICATIONS TO POLITICS** | |
| | 11 From Persons to Nations | 139 |
| | 12 Universal Man | 153 |
| | 13 Dynamic Diplomacy | 163 |
| *Part Five* | **CONCLUSION** | |
| | 14 Freedom to Be | 175 |
| | BIBLIOGRAPHY | 183 |
| | INDEX | 187 |

# Introduction

*Freedom to Be*

I am a unique person.
I must experience the world and express the person I am.
You are a unique person too.
You must experience and express yourself differently.
The experiencing and expressing of our total beings
Will find fulfillment in our appreciation of differences
and our mutual love.

Everett L. Shostrom

At the personal level, the above words represent the best way I am able to express the profound principle that I cannot be yourself for you and that you cannot be myself for me. Each of us is a unique entity and each of us must have the *Freedom to Be* himself. In contrast to B. F. Skinner, for me, man without freedom and dignity is nothing! The goal of therapy, and I believe of education, ought to be the experiencing and expressing of our total beings. *Freedom to Be* occurs when man is free to express himself, openly and completely on the polarities of anger-love and strength-weakness. *Freedom to Be* is my synonym for Actualization Therapy in process.

*Freedom to Be* is defined as man, in the here-and-now, daring to be himself, fully and freely. The *Freedom to Be* means trusting our total being in harmony: trusting our strength, trusting our weakness, trusting our anger and trusting our love. The *Freedom to Be* means finding the wisdom that all four express in unity.

For most of us, it is most difficult to trust the wisdom of our bodies. My feet tell me when I have "cold feet" or fears. My jaw and neck and shoulders tell me when I am "up tight" and resentful. My legs tell me what I "stand" for. My heart tells me when

## Introduction

I love and my eyes tell me when I am sad and hurt. This orientation requires no "shoulds," no "have to's," no rights and wrongs, but simply being what my organism is. It is elusive, but exciting, and this is the way I "know myself."

To learn to listen to our body is to accept that we *are* our bodies, not that we *have* a body. To be our organismic self is the *Freedom to Be*.

Manipulations or defenses are resistances to the *Freedom to Be* in which we play "roles" rather than being ourselves. Being what we feel, even our manipulations, leads to an expression of ourselves, whatever the response of others. Too often we say, "I didn't get a *response*." "I didn't make an *impact*." "I didn't make an *impression*." "It did no good to talk." "He doesn't understand." "He didn't buy it." We measure the success of our interaction by what "works," by how successful we are in manipulating the other into our way of thinking.

We measure our worth by the external affirmation of others, rather than by our internal trust in self-expression. Our current music expresses this notion of inner trust. Sammy Davis sings "I've got to be me; I can't be right for anyone else if I'm not right for me." Frank Sinatra also sings "I've got to do it 'My Way'." Jimmy Rogers sings "I want to be Free."

This leads to the *paradox of growth*. Change comes from being what we are and not trying to become something other than we are. Only when we stop trying to change and simply be ourselves will authentic change or growth come about. Change or growth comes from being, not trying to be something or somebody we are not.

I want to make it very clear that I do not regard the *Freedom to Be* or actualization as some *static goal* or *state of being* to which we all someday wish to aspire. *Freedom to Be,* for me, is rather a *process* of dynamic being in the here-and-now in which realities and goals are constantly changing. Only a person who is tuned to constant change and growth is **actual**izing or is free. Otherwise, he is tied to the rigid patterns of the past or to the inflexible goals of the future.

It seems to me that teenagers, women's liberationists, blacks, browns, and yellows, in fact, all persons, are asking for the *Free-

## Introduction

*dom to Be* their own uniqueness, and not simply to be a second-class citizen.

At the international level, the *Freedom to Be* is equally and profoundly significant. President Nixon, in his historic confrontation with Premier Chou of China, said the following:

> We begin our talks recognizing that we have great differences between us, but we are determined that those differences will not prevent us from living together in peace.
>
> You believe deeply in your system, and we believe just as deeply in our system. It is not our common beliefs that have brought us together here but our common interest and our common hopes. *

The ability to comprehend the significance of this new doctrine, at both the personal and international levels, is most important. What is being said here is that no longer can we relate as persons or as countries at the "missionary level of interaction," where we either meet as friends with common beliefs or we try then to convert the other to our way of thinking. We must relate as persons or as countries to say what is inside of ourselves, to express our unique selves, and our unique values. *Expression is not to change or convince another person or another country*. Expression is to *express*, not to *impress*. Only when the *"expression* level of interaction" replaces the *missionary* level will we be able to live not only with differences in the world, but to *appreciate those differences*. The future of our world depends to some extent on understanding this idea.

In addition to the concept of individual uniqueness, the *Freedom to Be* or actualizing rests on the expression of *polarities*. Polarities give us a road map for being our strengths and our weaknesses, our anger and our love.

A primary principle here is that most things are related to a zero-point from which a differentiation takes place into polar opposites. Such opposites or polarities show a great affinity for each other. For example, in color psychology, green represents a

* (*Los Angeles Times,* p. 10, part 1, Feb. 26, 1972)

zero point from which yellow and blue differentiate into polarities. Purple is a zero point from which blue and red differentiate into polarities. By remaining in the center, we can rhythmically relate to both sides without becoming fixated on one side only. It is the opposite of taking a narrow, one-sided outlook. Each person is like a bouquet of multicolored flowers. We are similar to others, but each of us is unique, individual, and irreplaceable.

The concept of polarities is solidly grounded on research done by Leary, Coffey, Barron, and others (17) of the Kaiser Foundation Psychology Research Group at Berkeley, and also deeply rooted in Eastern thought. In order for growth to take place, one must be aware of the polarities in oneself, in one's values, and in human interaction. Polarities must not simply be seen as oppositions or conflicts, but rather internal differences to assist man in his own growth and awareness.

The polarities of life are a rarely understood phenomenon. Man usually assumes there is conflict or opposition within himself and others, and between man and society. Even Freud accepted this traditional belief. Man, to him, was fundamentally antisocial and society must fight to domesticate him. Many young people today make the same error in assuming an irreconcilable conflict between the "establishment" and themselves.

The truth of living appears to be that apparently contradictory tendencies aren't contradictory at all, but can be seen as two aspects of a dialectical process which can be reconciled to be parts of a greater third thing or "Tertium Quid."

Another way of saying this is that for every truth, there is an equal and opposite counter-truth. The reconciliation of differences is the art of living. In Britain, the opposition party is known as "Her Majesty's *loyal* opposition." In physics, it is like appreciating the "pull" from both sides of the magnet. In Oriental philosophy, it is the appreciation of both Ying and Yang. In America, it means valuing both Democrats and Republicans, both youth and age, etc.

Thinking in polarities rather than simply in opposites is the mark of the actualizing person. Right–Wrong, Good–Bad, Ours–Theirs, are opposites which confuse because they are either–or, and not integrative. Lao-Tze, the great Chinese philosopher, says

*Introduction*

"It is the *concern* for right and wrong which is the sickness of the mind." * This leads to a rejection of our supposed "Bad Self" and creates an internal civil war, leaving us split into being only half our potential. Appreciation of the polarities within ourselves leads to accepting the *whole-someness* of our selves, and avoids the trap of rigid thinking.

Just as in Gestalt psychology, the two sides of the coin, or figure and ground must always go together, so the individual derives his identity from the reconciliation and integration of the polarities within himself.

What this really means is that each of us must trust his own organism or "Inner Supreme Court." This does not mean ignoring society, but struggling to integrate the conflicting values we face. I believe that most of our struggles come in inner conflicts with the polarities of strength-weakness and anger-love. For example, most of us are taught to "Stand up and be counted," and yet we are also told, "Blessed are the meek." We are admonished to "Love our neighbor," and yet that we must not "let the sun set on our wrath."

Our struggle in trying to integrate our polarities is the unique task of discovering the truth of our own beings. It requires a deeply spiritual attitude in which the self is our body and is regarded as a trustworthy homeostatic control system. To affirm this about oneself is to have the most profound faith in one's total being.

A primary tenet of this volume is the deepest commitment to the wisdom of man's total being. Man, seeking to survive, has often trusted his intelligence or head, and denied the feelings of his body. Bleuler (4) has said schizophrenia is the inability to modulate affect. I say actualization is the ability to modulate affect. Pascal has said, "The heart (one's feelings) has reasons which reason will never know." Intellectualizing without emotionalizing results in deadness rather than aliveness. The *Freedom to Be* is the freedom to integrate our thinking *and* our feeling—to be fully *there* in the moment—to personally experience that *"Freedom to Be* means 'It's Fun to Be Me!'"

\* Emphasis added.

# Part One

# THEORY

# 1

## The Uncharted Course

Our entire economy in the United States appears aimed at an easier and more satisfying life. Medicine has struggled to reduce pain and prolong life. Modern technology has invaded the factory and the kitchen, the golf course and outer space, to provide man with greater comforts and to open new frontiers. Yet something is wrong.

Our path through life is not an easy route. Life is a vast, uncharted territory through which we must break trail, backing and detouring at times, moving forward purposefully when we find a clear passage. When astronauts venture into space, braving the uncertainties that lie ahead, they live in their comparatively short trek through the celestial wilderness an encapsulated version of their total life experience. They are explorers, as we too must be if we are to achieve complete fulfillment.

I believe that hardship and frustration are essential qual-

## Theory

ities of human life. In our search for personal maturation, pain is the very condition of growth. We must learn to enjoy the discomfort of striving.

Some of our young people reject that vision of life, however; they are "easy riders" who propose to conquer the adult world by peacefully manipulating parents who are all too willing to be manipulated. Quite often mothers and fathers do not want conflict and confrontation; they see life as a process of finding the path of least resistance.

Reality means different things to different people. Dr. Frederick S. Perls (33)[*], the renowned Gestalt therapist, describes his idea of reality in this now famous passage:

> I do my own thing, and you do your thing.
> I am not in this world to live up to your expectations
> And you are not in this world to live up to mine.
> You are you and I am I.
> And if by chance we find each other, it's beautiful.
> If not, it can't be helped.

Dr. Perls, my teacher and therapist, achieved wide recognition, especially among the younger generation, with this philosophy. Yet I feel it does not go nearly far enough in the theory of interpersonal relationships. With all due respect to Dr. Perls, "doing your own thing" is not enough; we cannot risk *not* seeking out those "significant others"—parents and children, sisters and brothers, husbands and wives—in our lives; we cannot risk leaving such meetings to chance and simply regretting their absence. Independence is not *my* thing. For me, full reality is *interdependence*. To achieve this goal requires risking, *seeking out,* and communicating with others.

[*] Numbers refer to Bibliography listings.

## The Uncharted Course

Interdependence is a prerequisite to full maturity, a state which, paradoxically, involves continuously facing our choices with those we love. Or to put the last two lines another way:

> If by chance we meet and *choose* to be together
> We will experience the fulfillment of mutual love.

Alan Watts (51) has pointed out that man is not a fixed and separate ego, but part of the dancing pattern of energy that makes up the network of nature. Each of us is a complex maze, an arabesque of tubes, filaments, cells, fibers, and membranes; each of us is part of a network of natural patterns. This is ecology: the recognition that man is interdependent with all of life. To destroy or ignore this fact is to destroy oneself. When we *accept* the fact of our interdependence, only then are we fully evolving.

If either dependence or independence is considered as an end in itself, the result will be a failure to understand what life is really all about. For example, if *dependence* means happiness, then Joleen, a tall, natural honey-blonde, would have lived out her courtship and marriage in supreme ecstasy. As we shall see, she did not.

Joleen met her future husband, Lou, while both were in their senior year as undergraduates at the University of California at Los Angeles. They decided that they would marry after graduation, and that she would work to support them while he earned his law degree. They quickly established a marked dependence on one another. Lou needed her to survive physically, and Joleen—a shy girl despite her beauty—needed him to survive emotionally.

Trouble began almost immediately. On her wedding night Joleen found that she had great difficulty in achieving orgasm. As she later explained shyly to our sensitivity group,

## Theory

she had entered the marriage a virgin. "I wasn't even sure what to *do*," she lamented.

Lou was well versed in the ways of physical sex and considered her apparent lack of response a threat to his manhood; his failure to understand her dilemma turned their wedding night into a bizarre Marat-Sade type of confrontation. Aroused, he had an early climax as she clutched him lovingly. "I knew that something had happened to him that hadn't happened to me," she later told the group. "I mean I could *feel* that; but it didn't matter. It honestly didn't matter." She was very happy just to be his chosen partner.

It may not have mattered to Joleen, but it quickly became clear that it mattered a great deal to Lou. He took her in his arms.

"Did you?" he whispered.

"Did I what?"

"Have an orgasm?"

"No," she told him. "I don't think so."

They made love a second time for fifteen minutes—a steady, demanding fifteen minutes that began to tire her. He asked her if she was "ready."

"I . . . I don't think so," she whispered.

His motion was now more demanding than loving. She was aroused and kept up with him for many minutes, but again tired and assumed a more passive role. Lou, of course, immediately sensed her diminished participation. Now tense in a way that she sensed had nothing to do with their physical coupling, he grew hostile.

"What's the matter with you?"

"I don't know, Lou." She felt as though she might cry, but knew that would be the wrong thing to do.

A suggestion of desperation entered his lovemaking.

"Lou, darling," she pleaded. "You're hurting me."

"I'm sorry." He was repentant but didn't stop.

"*You* do it, honey," she said. "I'm fine."
"No."
"Please," she whispered. "It's all right."
"It's *not* all right." His tone was harsh.
She bit her lip to force back the tears.
"*I* won't come if you won't," he said fiercely.
"Please, Lou . . ."
He withdrew suddenly, leaving her shocked and exposed. "What are you trying to prove?" he demanded angrily. "That you're some kind of a super sexpot?" When Joleen finished telling her experience to the group she was in tears as she had been on that traumatic first night.

The young couple's "need" for one another continued to keep them together in the same small, off-campus apartment, but they were both becoming more and more unstable emotionally. Try as he could, Lou could not bring her to orgasm. Their sexual relationship became first a challenge and then a despair to them both. She felt more and more inadequate as Lou punished her verbally for her supposed failure in bed. She began to feel that his refusal to complete the act was the result of her inadequacy. Unhappy and disillusioned, she sought the help of a psychiatrist who told her that the problem stemmed from her sexual frigidity—when in fact it was her husband's hostility that was making their relationship so difficult. Because Lou depended on Joleen for his economic survival, he had to express his manhood by making her feel inferior. For her part, Joleen simply needed to be needed. "I don't want just to be a vagina to him," she told me.

What she failed to understand was that he was not even *honestly* using her as a pleasure outlet. He had to be a man —and to him, that meant putting her down, punishing her for supporting him. As we will see, she in turn built up a great hostility toward her husband.

## Theory

"The psychiatrist kept asking me to disregard what was happening to me now," Joleen confided to our group, "and asked me to return to the 'neurotic core' of my problem. He began asking me if I felt any 'erotic transference' to himself of my feelings for my husband."

Although Joleen was in her late twenties by the time she abandoned Freudian analysis and came to me, she was locked in the first stage of what I like to think of as a three-stage growth process toward emotional maturity. Her childlike *dependence* had little to do with chronological age; some people never outgrow it. As I wrote in *Man, the Manipulator*, a child—whether he or she is eight or twenty-eight—can be highly manipulative. Manipulation is *artificial* pressure. By making her husband financially dependent on her, Joleen was indeed exercising a form of manipulation, getting him into a situation where he would feel obligated to her.

But Lou was practicing a far more subtle and potentially more damaging manipulation, much as a parent might do to a child. Lou was like the parent unwilling to allow a child freedom to grow beyond the initial stage of dependency, unwilling to let Joleen move forward because he feared that her journey into *independence*, the second stage of our growth process, would take her away from his control.

Before we follow Joleen through her interesting journey through *independence* to the ultimate actualizing state of *interdependence*, I would like briefly to discuss the "now" generation of psychotherapy as it is currently evolving at our Institute.

Joleen was disillusioned with her psychiatrist, but she did not know exactly why. This does not mean, of course, that all psychiatrists employ outmoded therapeutic techniques any more than that all psychologists are the self-actualizing heralds of a brave new world of vigorous, continuous evolvement. It does mean that many of the traditional methods of analysis must stand the scrutiny of an advancing society. If they are found wanting, then therapists must move the couch back and make room for chairs so that patients can sit up straight, without having first to regress into a stultifying limbo of past hurts and pains. I *have* found the old therapeutic ways wanting. Many psychiatrists, by the very nature of their medical training, tend to look for symptoms of disease in emotional as well as organic disorders. Freudian psychoanalysis, with its emphasis on the patient's past history, is a natural adjunct of this essentially negative approach.

In Actualization Therapy, rather, we say: "Let's assume reasonable health. Let's concern ourselves with what is happening to us *now* and go on from here to realize our full potential as human beings." The fact that we have problems does not mean that we are ill. One of my colleagues at the Institute put it very simply during a University of California extension course held in one of our lecture halls: "We are persons here, not patients," he said. "This course [on actualization therapy] is simply the beginning of a journey that may last a lifetime."

When Joleen joined one of our sensitivity groups, she began that journey and soon found that it was not going to be all smooth sailing. "An individual human existence," the eminent philosopher Bertrand Russell wrote in his *Portraits From Memory* (37), "should be like a river—small at first, narrowly contained within its banks, and rushing passionately past boulders and over waterfalls. Gradually the river grows wider, the banks recede, the waters flow more quietly, and in the end, without any visible break, they become merged in the sea, and painlessly lose their individual being."

The life journey, which is so difficult when undertaken alone, is eased considerably in the actualizing atmosphere of our encounter groups. Actualizing in this context is the process, to continue with Lord Russell's aqueous analogy, of

## Theory

moving from dog-paddler to Australian crawler during our downstream journey. When we reach the sea and painlessly lose our individual being in the "becoming" of *interdependence,* we should be swimming strongly beside others who, while respecting our water-space, choose to match us stroke for stroke.

By the time Joleen despaired of ever finding relief in sex-oriented analysis and joined my group, Lou had barely graduated from law school and was attempting to build a successful practice. His outside life, which she was certain included other women, had pulled them further apart. She had borne him one son, but was very unhappy with her lot. Lou left her to vegetate at home. Once or twice she had mentioned the possibility of their separating, and each time he had asked her to reconsider because, "That sort of thing would look bad at this stage of my career."

As often happens, Joleen—a newcomer to the eight-person group—did not participate to any great extent during the first two or three sessions that she attended. I agree with my colleague at the United States International University, Dr. Viktor Frankl, that a group therapist's role should be akin to that of a guide on a dangerous mountain climbing expedition: he must hold the tethering rope, but loosely so that any two people can rescue a third. For this reason my own contribution to the group took the form of keeping the members on what I considered to be productive paths and of emphasizing (subtly, I trust) how urgent it was for them to arrive at an *interdependence* that would enable them to relate meaningfully to others, to know and experience other people not because of need but through choice.

Ostensibly I was exchanging thoughts and ideas with the whole group, but actually I was addressing myself to Joleen and her problems. I hoped that while she watched the others act out their uncertainties and frustrations, she would ex-

*The Uncharted Course*

perience the urge to commit herself. That is the key to any successful therapy, just as it is the key to a successful life: the determination to take a chance, to stick one's emotional neck out, to know uncertainty and to explore the unknown with the full knowledge that temporary setbacks may crop up.

Finally, hesitantly, Joleen spoke about her husband. I encouraged her with a question:

"How do you really feel about Lou?"

"I . . . I don't know."

"You don't know or you won't say?" I persisted.

Joleen smiled. "A little of both, I guess."

"Do you see how you're sitting? Up straight with your back tensed and your hands clasped in front of you?"

She shifted uncomfortably. "No. I didn't notice."

"You're angry at something. You're so angry that you can hardly contain yourself."

"Yes," she said submissively.

"Who are you angry at?"

"Lou."

I pulled a heavy glass ashtray over and set it before her on the coffee table. "There's Lou. Tell him what you're thinking. Begin your sentences with 'I resent . . .'"

Joleen looked up from the ashtray with an embarrassed smile, saw that the group was waiting expectantly, looked back down at the ashtray, swallowed, then addressed the surrogate husband.

"I resent *you*."

"I can't hear you."

"I resent you. I resent you making me feel inadequate."

"You're intellectualizing," I put in. "Tell him what you really feel. Your real feelings."

"I resent your playing around." She clenched her fists. "I resent your superiority. I *hate* your superiority."

## Theory

"Louder."

"I hate your superiority! I resent working all that time so you can go out and make love to some bitch." She was trembling now. "I hate the whole goddamn mess we're in."

"Him. How do you feel about him?"

Joleen stared at the ashtray, tears welling up in her eyes. "I *hate* you."

"Louder."

"I *hate* you!"

"Louder."

"*I hate you.*" Sobbing now, she buried her face in her hands, spent as she never had been after the sex act. Around the room people exhaled slowly as someone handed Joleen a tissue.

The ice was broken. Joleen looked relaxed and said that she felt better as a result of her outburst. She went on much more calmly to recount the situation described in the beginning of this chapter and, for the first time, felt the wonderful interpersonal group warmth that comes only with total commitment.

No one had to tell Joleen that life is often painful and challenging. What she did not yet understand was that she had begun the lengthy, exciting progression toward "growing well" through the actualizing process. Emotionally speaking, Joleen was going somewhere, and as we shall see in the succeeding chapters, an alive person going somewhere is the most exhilirating example of a meaningful life. For Joleen, life had simply meant existence; now she would begin to experience living. Life had driven her before it; now she would do the driving. Life had meant only survival; now she would take some risks.

She is not alone. I believe that *interdependence,* the choosing to live with others, to appreciate their differences and to value those very differences, is fast becoming an international

## The Uncharted Course

way of life. What we experience in the privacy of our group is being duplicated a thousandfold, albeit without the conscious knowledge of the participants, in the relationships between the states of our union and of that union to the nations of the world. This is a complex movement that is at the same time as simple as what happens between two human beings in intimate contact.

# 2

## Survival vs. Growth

In an address to the United Nations General Assembly, President Richard Nixon spoke of the United States' peacekeeping role after World War II. "For much of the world," the President said, "those first, difficult postwar years were a time of *dependency*. The next step was toward *independence*, as new nations were born and old nations revived. Now we are maturing together into a new pattern of *interdependence*." (All italics mine.)

The President is an example of what I refer to as a *growth-oriented* individual. In his book *Toward a Psychology of Being* (23), the humanistic psychologist Abraham Maslow speaks of the survival-oriented needs of safety, security, belongingness, and love. Surely Richard Nixon began his career with the satisfaction of many of these needs uppermost in his existence. His humble beginnings, his service in Congress, in the Armed Forces, in the Senate, and, after his vice-presi-

*Theory*

dency, in the White House itself, were accompanied by quite natural survival needs. Unlike many of his predecessors who were born to wealth and the self-assurance that social position often brings, Nixon had to do it the hard way, to be other-directed, living in terms of others' demands.

Although always a growing individual—he could hardly have survived his two great political defeats, first for the presidency against John F. Kennedy, then for the governorship of California, if he were not—it is only since his election to our highest public office that he has truly been able to shake free of the independence that he first had to achieve, and to enter the growth-oriented, inner-directed world of interdependence. In the process, as the brief speech exerpt above indicates, he changed from politician to statesman.

Although we may never reach such a position of awesome responsibility, the stages that led Richard Nixon to the presidency apply equally, if in smaller measure, to each of us.

First of all, we must understand that a survival orientation develops because of our extreme dependence on our parents during childhood. Though well-intentioned, our parents bombard us with "shoulds" or "should nots" admonitions of how we must behave in terms of their standards. We never really lose this *survival-orientation,* but we can develop another set of *growth-orientation* values that will enable us to become full-functioning, to actualize our potential.

For the sake of simplicity I have reduced the forces involved to four basic modalities. Taking a cross section from hundreds of cases through my more than twenty years in practice, I have isolated "Love-Anger" and "Strength-Weakness" as basic polarities relating to the survival and growth orientations. The following examples are, I feel, instructive:

*Survival vs. Growth*

# SURVIVAL

## Love Demands

"You should always love your brothers and sisters."

"Come and kiss your mother."

"You should never feel sexy."

"You better do what I want."

## Anger Demands

"You should never be nasty."

"You should control your temper."

"Don't you ever blow up like that again."

# GROWTH

## Love Expressions

"I love you even though there are things about you I don't like."

"I care deeply for you, even if I don't feel it in return."

"I feel sexually toward you, and much more: affection, empathy, and appreciation."

"I love you because I choose to, not because I have to."

## Anger Expressions

"Sometimes I feel so angry that I'd like to choke you. I won't actually *do* it, but I *feel* it."

"My resentment toward you is very strong right now."

"I just hate you right now."

*Theory*

"You better do what I want."

"I feel righteous about my indignation toward you."

## Weakness Demands

"Don't show your tender side."

"Don't you cry!"

"Don't ever let anybody get to you."

"Boys don't feel weak, only girls do that."

## Weakness Expressions

"I feel open and vulnerable."

"I want to cry now."

"I'm very aware of my imperfections."

"I really want to surrender to you."

## Strength Demands

"Don't you ever defy me!"

"Don't think too much of yourself."

"Always be humble."

"Don't be proud or something bad will happen."

## Strength Expressions

"I feel really adequate now."

"I am a capable psychologist."

"I can do it well."

"I am strong—whether you feel it or not."

*Survival vs. Growth*

We live in constant danger of not being our natural, growing selves because of our dependence on our parents or the authorities who make the demands in the left hand column of the foregoing list. Indeed, we often depend on demanding persons for our very survival; instead of expressing our natural feelings, we distort our reactions and develop manipulative processes to appease them. We stop being naturally loving, angry, strong, or weak; instead we concoct manipulative expressions of these extremes that are *safe,* that do not threaten our survival.

Instead of loving we become safely placating, instead of being genuinely angry, we simply blame. Instead of being genuinely strong, we connive to control indirectly. Instead of admitting that we feel genuinely weak and impotent, we withdraw so as not to show our vulnerability. In order to survive, we develop manipulative response forms that appease the authorities in our life.

# Manipulative Response Forms

The four basic "Manipulative Response Forms" are shown diagrammatically in Figure 1. The first manipulative process begins when a child learns that the best way he can cope with life is to placate his parents and others—to please them by erasing his own personality, since he feels "It's not okay to be me." This first manipulative pattern involves reducing one's own significance. As adults we usually do it by being either a "Nice Guy" or a "Protector." The "Nice Guy" says, "No matter what happens, I'll always be nice to you. *I* don't count, *you* count." The "Protector" pattern has become familiar through the stereotype of the Jewish mother: "My *children* count. I'm going to care for you, be good to you, *sacrifice myself* for you."

# MANIPULATIVE RESPONSE FORMS

Fig. 1

## Survival vs. Growth

Early in life the child makes the assumption that it is better to trust the parents' wishes for himself than to trust his own body. He decides that the better option is to manipulate his body in order to please his parents.

I believe that all manipulative forms of behavior are felt to be creative by the person engaging in the behavior. What the child is doing in this case is denying his *anger,* which we recognize to be the opposite of the behavioral pattern he has chosen. He often manipulates his body to do this. He tightens the muscles of his neck, shoulders, and jaw to deny his hostility. It is only a short step from this sort of bodily manipulation of self to the interpersonal manipulation of others.

Blaming is the second manipulative process that we learn. Instead of being self-destructive, we choose the reverse: we attack and criticize others. Our problems must be blamed on someone else. The blamer may be a "Bully" who tries to strong-arm everyone into admitting he is right, or he may play the "Judge," preaching to others what they should be and where they have gone wrong.

As Figure 1 shows, the placating and blaming processes represent opposite ways of manipulating—one by erasing the self, the other by demolishing someone else. As with all other manipulative processes, we learn these from parents or authority figures.

Again, however, notice the creative dimenson. Just as the placator denies his anger, the blamer too must deny what he feels to be the opposite of the behavioral role he has chosen. Thus he denies his tender or loving feelings. To love is to be hurt; therefore it is better to attack. He manipulates his body. His stomach tightens, he tenses his vital organs for attack, and takes the offensive. Life becomes a battle for survival.

The third manipulative response is the conniving process,

## Theory

represented by the "Calculator" and the "Dictator." The conniver has learned that the way to survive is to have a plan or scheme of living: "It really doesn't matter what *I* count for or what *you* count for: it's *controlling the situation* that is important, and to do that I must plan and scheme." Thus the "Dictator" says that the only thing that matters is the good of the group, and he will tell them what that "good" is and how to achieve it. The "Calculator" is similar but sneakier—he tries to get you to accept his ideas. The father who sells his kids on going to college and the used car salesman both pay little attention to the wishes of the people involved and care only about making a sale.

Once again, the creativity of this solution is apparent, for the conniver has learned that he must deny his weakness, which is the opposite polarity from the pattern he has chosen. His method keeps this vulnerability carefully hidden. A supersalesman's or a dictatorial parent's "puffed chest" are physical manifestations of personal as well as of interpersonal control.

Avoiding is the fourth manipulative process shown in Figure 1. The avoider withdraws from himself, from others, and from any troubling situation, so that nothing matters. The weakling says, "I can't do it—I give up!" The clinging vine depends on others to think and act for him; he says, "I can't do it—*you* do it." The avoider has learned to believe that he cannot do anything on his own, so he has stopped trying.

The creative power of the avoider's weakness must not be overlooked. The avoider has found that by pleading innocence and weakness, he can seduce others to do his job. He has denied his *strength*, the opposite of his manipulative style. His physical makeup reflects this chosen style of coping with life; the avoider is usually a skinny-legged person who does not hear or see well even though he has no hearing and seeing defect. He has creatively learned not to look and listen!

The research by Leary and others (17) has shown that the basic polarities are universal; that when over 5000 cases are tested, these dimensions describe a fully-functioning being. Our very existence requires us to deal with the two basic polarities of Love versus Anger and Strength versus Weakness. But yet in attempting to cope with life, we deny the necessity of coping with one or more of these dimensions. We deny or block the dimension of being that opposes our chosen life-style. As Albert Pesso (34) has shown, our childlike or primitive reasoning does not allow for bipolar thinking. Thus as children we think in terms of yes or no, good or bad, and as we grow older we tend to choose one way and to deny its alternative. The lover denies his anger, the blamer denies his love, the conniver denies his weakness, and the weakling denies his strength.

The growth process, on the other hand, involves considerable awareness. It requires an awareness of *how* we manipulate our bodies as well as *how* we manipulate other people. This, in turn, suggests two processes: individual analysis and group therapy. In individual therapy we help a person to see his basic style of body functioning, and in group therapy the resulting interpersonal manipulations become apparent.

Returning to the case of Joleen and Lou with these considerations in mind, we can see that Joleen and Lou were waging their own intense struggle to achieve a satisfactory interpersonal relationship. Despite the deeply ingrained parental domination that made her shy and reticent, we can easily imagine Joleen striving to speak our third Growth-oriented Love Expression to her husband: "I feel sexually toward you," she would tell him, "and much more: affection, empathy, and appreciation."

*Theory*

But—and here we become apprehensive that Lou is driving them both irretrievably into independence—her husband can respond only with our second Survival-oriented Weakness Demand. "Don't you cry!" he orders her, because her crying out in frustration and fear threatens him and makes him even more uncertain of his manhood.

In a private session, Lou assured me quite confidently that he appreciated everything that Joleen had done for him, but he was making it on his own now and simply did not need her. From what Joleen had told me, I knew that in fact he had called her quite often, that he had arranged to keep picking up his mail at her place (a patently manipulative act), and that he appeared lonely. I asked Lou about his love life.

"Have you found another girl?"

He fidgeted. "No. Not really. I've taken out a couple but it didn't go any further."

"How do you feel toward Joleen?"

He shrugged. "I can't communicate with her. As a matter of fact, she bugs me."

"You feel that you don't need her."

"Yeah." He looked down at the floor. "Yeah, that's it."

"You feel strong as far as she's concerned."

Lou became slightly antagonistic. "I don't feel strong and I don't feel weak." He twisted in his chair. "I just don't need her."

"I don't think you feel strong."

"How do you mean?"

"We must show our weakness before we can realize our strength."

Lou was visibly disturbed. "I don't know what you're talking about."

"Will you try something with me?" I asked.

Lou shrugged and said that he didn't see why not. I asked

him to lie full length on the floor on his back. I knelt beside him, placing my hand on his abdomen and pressing down firmly. I urged him to relax, but it was obvious that he was tense and nervous.

"Breathe with your stomach against my hand. Not with your lungs, with your diaphragm."

He breathed and I pressed. It does not take very long before one feels a sense of physical weakness after breathing like that against pressure. Lou soon relaxed. He was tired, and his deep breathing had made him more in touch with his feelings. I raised myself and held my right hand about three feet over his now perspiring face. He looked up at me as I continued, speaking softly.

"Do you feel relaxed?"

"Tired."

"It's a good feeling, isn't it?"

"Yes."

"You can let go."

"Yes."

"I'm here to help you."

"I don't know . . ."

"Let go. Ask me for help."

After some effort Lou said, "I . . . I can't."

Quietly, patiently, I told him "Don't be afraid to ask."

"I'm not . . ." He broke off, visibly in distress. Then, after a pause, he said slowly, "Will . . . will you help me?"

"Again."

His voice quavered. "Help me . . ."

"That's it. Again."

His eyes were beseeching, and moist. "Help me . . ."

"Again."

*"Help me."*

It came out in a torrent of emotion as tears ran unashamedly down his cheeks. He reached up impulsively and

## Theory

grabbed my outstretched hand as he kept repeating "Help me" over and over again. For the moment, he had lost all self-control. It was an exhausting, but highly rewarding experience. Emotionally, as well as physically drained, Lou marveled at his heretofore unrealized capacity for "letting down." For a brief time he had permitted himself freely to express his honest feelings.

I had no illusions that this brief episode would magically clear up his and Joleen's problems, but I did feel that it was at least one small step toward actualization. Lou had managed to shed the controlled ingrained, survival-oriented habits of a lifetime and, in so doing, had given them both hope in allowing himself to feel his genuine weakness for the first time.

I cannot overemphasize how therapy alters when it is humanistically, rather than pathologically, oriented. When a person views himself as a patient, he thinks of himself as sick, stupid, sinful, impotent. As a *growing person,* on the other hand, he becomes responsible, potent, and eager to learn how he can become even more creative while coping with life. This "new humanistic view" of therapy is based upon a more optimistic view of man's nature than either psychoanalysis or psychiatry. Psychiatry has too long stressed that life is sickness rather than search, avoidance rather than adventure.

Everywhere there are medicine manholes ready to trap the unwary in the dark depths of mental illness. The new view sees that man has a "possible dream" for himself—that life can focus on ascent rather than descent.

We develop a *passion for ascent,* an expressing of our individuality, a reaching out for ultimate meaning, and a drive to communicate our love and responsibility. As mountain climbers are responsible for each other, so the adventurer is interdependent in his orientation, his rope tied loosely to his partner for safety, yet allowing freedom for them both to move independently as they journey together to actualization.

## The Growth Alternative

As children, all of us "sell out" to the Survival Orientation. The important thing is that we discover the alternative Growth Orientation, but the learning process requires risk and time. It requires that we learn clearly the alternatives to manipulation: loving, being genuinely angry, feeling our strength honestly, and risking our weaknesses openly. In spite of our childhood deficiencies, I believe these growth options can be learned in individual and group therapy, and I intend, in succeeding chapters, to show examples of how this can be accomplished.

# 3

## Tertium Quid

It is misleading to think of the personal growth-oriented journey as a straight, unbroken line upward. D. H. Lawrence (16), in his *Apocalypse,* observed:

> Our idea of time as a continuity in an eternal straight line has crippled our consciousness cruelly. The pagan conception of time as moving in cycles is much freer, it allows for a complete change of the state of mind, at any moment. One cycle finished, we can drop or rise to another level, and be in a new world at once. But by our time-continuum method, we have to trail wearily on over another ridge.

Laymen and professionals alike have made much of the so-called "generation gap" and, indeed, the nature of our social structure has changed along with our cultural values. We

*Theory*

must not forget, however, that values, implicit or explicit, still create that structure. The psychologist Warren Bennis (3) sees the shift in cultural values from the last generation to this in the following terms:

| From | Toward |
|---|---|
| Self-control | Self-actualization |
| Independence | Interdependence |
| Endurance of stress | Capacity for joy |
| Full employment | Full lives |
| Mechanistic forms | Organic forms |
| Competitive relations | Collaborative relations |

I like to think that man's inner journey is being guided by the set of values in the right-hand column.

To follow Lawrence's analogy, the road that we take is full of plateaus, peaks, and valleys. Sometimes whole lives seem to be lived on plateaus—for example, the late Eleanor Roosevelt, who was a realist with a continuing, unbroken devotion to duty and an unswerving sense of obligation toward her fellow man. Similarly, the self-actualizing English novelist, essayist, and satirist Aldous Huxley was a "peak" person who found everything, to use his favorite expression, "Extraordinary!"

Most people cannot live their whole lives on the plateaus. The majority of us (myself included) experience more than our share of *nadir* or "valley" experiences. Ernest Hemingway was an outstanding example of brilliance constantly teetering on the brink of despair. But in my own life I have found that, paradoxically, we can grow from each valley of worry, inability, fear, hurt, pain, or frustration—*provided that we are willing to go through them.*

This, I believe, is the essence of the therapeutic process: to "go through" troubles rather than to leap across or avoid them. I call these nadirs "fertile voids." Facing our hopelessness helps us to discover new resources. The mature man uses his frustrations to propel himself along the journey toward self-actualization.

But where are we at any given moment on this ultimate trip between polarities? I feel strongly that our ability to report where we are is a measure of our success, and that our contact with reality consists of our ability to determine our position accurately.

## Tertium Quid Formuli

The Tertium Quid, a Latin expression derived from the Greek *triton ti*, meaning "a third something" which is an integration of two other things, perhaps best expresses my thoughts about the tremendous importance of viewing life as a continuous process rather than as a static, predetermined experience. Once again using our Love-Anger, Weakness-Strength polarities as bases for Figure 2, we find four new dimensions added.

I believe that polarities are the very basic nature of our existence, the reality of life itself. These polar links may be viewed as highways on which man moves out from the hub toward the unknown.

If we choose manipulation rather than movement, we become "stuck" on one of the highways and manifest at least the suggestion of an incipient neurosis. If we are stopped at any point between the four extremities, making that point the epicenter of the polarities, then we are engaged in manipulative behavior. We must relate to the true center of polarities—the hub of our Figure 2—rather than to any bi-

TERTIUM QUID DIMENSIONS

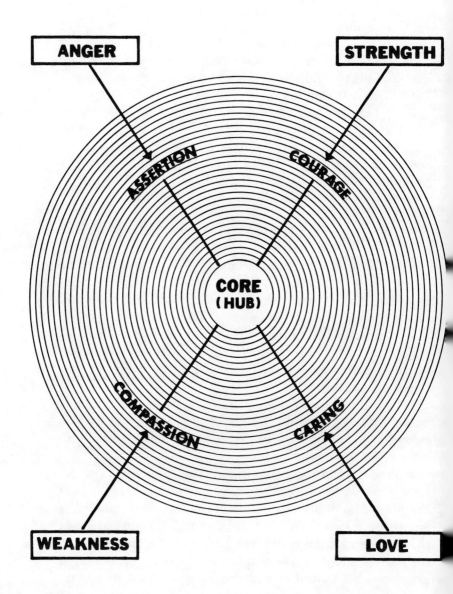

Fig. 2

ased, distorted view occasioned by a rigid inability to move back or forth.

If, for example, we become stuck on *Strength* we find ourselves power-oriented, unable to strike a proper balance in our relationships to others. The modern business executive, conscious only of his conglomerate hold over the destinies of many thousands of people, becomes (in his own mind) a benevolent despot, sure that he knows what is good for lesser mortals. But because of his locked-in manipulative stance, he is unable to communicate with them. Khrushchev, flirting with nuclear war because of his active encouragement of a Soviet presence on Cuba, is an outstanding modern example of the manipulative political adventurer so neatly characterized in the immediate past by Adolph Hitler and Joseph Stalin.

If we choose to wallow in *Weakness* and become self-manipulative to the point where we believe in our own impotence, we can easily assume the demeanor of a true schizoid. The "born loser" typifies the weakness-oriented manipulator. He plays upon other people's sympathy to gain his own ends. Most of us readily identify with him; television stars such as Don Knotts and Wally Cox have made careers of portraying his idiosyncracies.

Should we choose to walk around loaded with *Love,* we find ourselves practicing one of the most common and most transparent manipulative forms of *feigned* love. Who fails to spot the professional nice guy? The supercilious salesman, bent on foisting the latest model washing machine on our sagging bank accounts, is Mr. Nice, seemingly attentive to our every whim but actually viewing us in the harshest of lights. Sales mean survival to him, and if he has to love us to death to make them, so be it. The fawning waiter is another particularly obnoxious example of the love manipulation at work. Secretly he has sized us up and is trying to

## Theory

squeeze a little extra tip by generous applications of false servility. And it works! We buy his affection no matter how transient it may be.

Feeling and expressing only love, to the exclusion of anger, strength or weakness is also harmful. The wife, who denies her anger to show she "always" loves her husband becomes limited in her responsiveness. I believe people are like sandpaper and we all rub each other the wrong way sometimes. Then we have to say "ouch" and "I resent that." Unless you can say "no" sometimes, we cannot believe the perpetual "yes." Furthermore, love which denies strength lacks the power of real compassion.

Of course, if we find ourselves aroused to *Anger,* we end up using one of the most effective manipulative tools. Small angers build up over a period of time, and the result is an explosive hostility that permits no shadings of compassion or tolerance toward those around us. We collect resentments the way other people collect stamps or coins. When we feel that we have accumulated enough antagonisms, we spew them out in all directions, manipulating through intimidation.

So, being stalled on the outermost reaches of our Love-Anger, Weakness-Strength highways is not the answer. I believe that these polarities are essentially correlative, that they interact, and that our awareness of their interaction is the answer to a complete, fully realized existence.

Let us consider, then, the new dimension presented by the Tertium Quid in Figure 2.

Suppose, that instead of being stuck on Strength, we pry ourselves loose and venture, however timidly at first, down in the direction of weakness. Meeting weakness more than halfway, we suddenly find ourselves capable of relating to the central hub, the true center of our existence. No longer are we narrowly concentrated in an egocentric position that forces us to brutalize our relationship with others. Now we achieve a feeling of balance, a genuine *Courage* to face whatever life chooses to thrust our way and to deal with it in a mature manner by not being afraid to give of ourselves and our emotions.

In my opinion, the most significant question in psychotherapy is not "Who are you?" or "What are you?" but *"Where are you?"* The Tertium Quid permits us to answer this question, and in so doing it opens the door to a totally realized life pattern.

Let's resume our series of journeys, using Figure 2 as our roadmap. Suppose, instead of wallowing in Weakness, we set out boldly toward the hub or core that is our true center. We bump inevitably into strength, but it is a gentle bump of awareness that enables us to accept our true weakness while acknowledging our strengths. We experience *Compassion,* one of the most satisfying of human conditions. Compassion permits us to empathize with those around us without having to manipulate them; we understand ourselves and others and, in this understanding, become capable of true interdependence.

Now let us look at the loaded-with-Love types. If these people could see their way clear to travel but a few emotional miles along the highway toward the center they would find that some part of anger, the true expression of their emotions, awaits them. There they would experience the actualizing state of *Caring*. Instead of assaulting us with the hard sell, the salesman would genuinely care about which of his products is best for our needs. The waiter would minister to us not only because he expects a financial reward—a most natural motivation—but also because he takes real delight in seeing that we are well served and enjoy being in his presence. We meet examples of these actualizing people all the time, and life is so much the better for it; they make us feel good by their willingness to interact instead of manipulate.

If we find ourselves aroused to anger to the point where all sense of emotional balance is knocked aside, we are ready for a short vacation trip toward our center. Anger, expressed forcibly and repeatedly, denotes a lack of self-confidence. The hostile person feels that the best way to get out of an uncertain situation is to get mad at it, to belabor it until it goes away. The more we use this manipulative technique, the harder it is to start on our journey toward inner-directedness. As soon as we start down the polar highway we begin to feel the influence of approaching love; as we come closer to our correlative polarization, we feel more certain of ourselves until finally we are capable of *Assertion*. Our arrival at this point in our journey marks us as well balanced, emotionally stable individuals. Self-confident enough to be assertive but aware of our position in relation to the center of our polarities, we temper anger with love and arrive at a homeostatic emotional admixture.

Traditionally, psychotherapy has steered away from any suggestion of universal values. I believe this practice to be in error for the simple reason that man must orient himself to *something* if he is to stay sane. The four polarities of Weakness, Strength, Love, and Anger seem to me to come close to a concept of universal values, and their refinements of Compassion, Courage, Caring, and Assertion serve as vitally important orientation points from which man can perceive his relationship to those polarities.

# The Subjective Stance

In addition to inner-directedness, a primary characteristic of the Growth-Orientation is the Subjective Stance: The person sees himself primarily as an active "Subject" with choices, rather than a passive "Object" which is directed by the demands of others.

I believe it is quite clear that just as we can see a coin from either side, so we can view any event from an "objective" or from a more "subjective" view. It is not so much what happens to us, but the view we take of it which is important.

Fundamentally, this means that as persons we have the opportunity to take a stand, to view what happens either as an object—as something which is *acted upon,* or as a subject —a person who *acts.* The former is passive, the latter is active.

Basic English sentence structure is helpful here. In the sentence, "I get mad at *myself,*" there is the active "I" and the passive "myself" or "me" at which the "I" gets mad. When we say such a thing, we almost always identify with the passive "me." We are being "done to." We ignore the active "I" who is speaking, disowning active responsibility. If we are to take charge of our lives, we must become more active subjects—not simply passive and pathetic objects that get pushed around.

The danger of simply seeing oneself as a "me"—an object —rather than as an "I"—a subject—is inherent in the emotional state we call depression. One gets depressed when one turns one's anger on oneself. If a person denies that he is an "I" attacking a "me," then he simply accepts the self-punishment and becomes depressed and possibly suicidal. On the other hand, if that same person can accept his I-ness he will realize that he is the attacker as well as the attacked. Therapeutically this is very significant, for then it is possible to take one's subjective strength into oneself.

The change that I have in mind is best illustrated by a session that I had with Lou, when he and Joleen were still living together and his ego needs were making him very uneasy.

## Theory

"Lou, do you feel your father was more active and your mother passive?" I asked.

"Yes," Lou agreed.

"Be your father talking to your mother," I suggested.

"Okay, I'm father: 'Damn you, woman, I work hard all day and you sit on your duff and do nothing all day. Why don't you at least have my cocktail ready when I come home?' 'I'm sorry, darling, I just forgot.' 'Sorry, sorry, sorry, you're always sorry.' 'I know I goof a lot.' "

"Who do you identify with?" I put in.

"My mother, damn it."

"Can you feel your 'father self' more now?"

"Yes, and I like it. I feel stronger now."

Most of us need to identify more with our subject-selves and less with our object-selves. Our object-self feels controlled, directed; it describes its behavior with words like "have to," "must," "can't" and "should." These words—often used by parents to children—imply that we are under pressure from others and have to do what mother, father, husband, boss or—yes—therapist, wants us to. A subject feels free, able to act, and says what he "wants," "chooses," "prefers," and "feels."

We do not want to be *only* subjects, of course—sometimes it is good to be acted upon—but most of us need to feel our subjectness more than we do.

It is not easy for a person accustomed to self-manipulation to believe in his own subjectivity and to find out that he can *want, prefer, like, choose*. But if he can acquire a subjective way of looking at life, he will gain a sense of freedom, of being authentic, and responsible. One of the first steps toward actualization is to see ourselves as persons who have choices. As adults who are no longer in fact dependent on others, it is only our own view of ourselves that makes us think we lack freedom.

## Tertium Quid

We are free even to make wrong decisions. The wrong decision is often better than none. Sometimes it is even better than the "right" one, if the "right" one is not truly ours. We must realize that we never have to do anything we don't want to do, even if it is "right."

No nonpsychotic adult need say, "They won't let me do anything," or "You made me do it." Phrases like "I am," "I choose," "I want to" can help us learn to accept responsibility by reminding us that we really do choose life for ourselves.

For most people, independence begins as early as the ages of two to three-and-a-half years (the "no" stage), and comes to full bloom in adolescence. But many allow themselves to be manipulated even in adulthood, remaining dependent on others when it is no longer necessary. The beauty of life is that we can catch up—we are given second chances to see ourselves as subjects.

Rollo May (26), writing about himself, vividly illustrates how the subjective view of oneself is necessary for real creativity:

> I sit here writing. . . . As I work I experience myself as a man who has to get a chapter done, who has set himself a deadline. . . . I find the uncomfortable thought pressing in, "My colleague, Professor So-and-So, will not like this point; perhaps I should obfuscate my idea a little—make it sound profound and not so easy to attack?" . . .
>
> I am viewing and treating myself as an object. . . . Note that my sentences hinge on such verbs as *have to, must*. . . . I treat myself as one who must "fit in"; I am gratified at the moment that I am a creature of habit without much leeway in behavior; and my aim is to make this leeway even less, to control my behavior more rigidly. . . .

*Theory*

> But as I continue writing, I find myself suddenly caught up in an interesting idea. . . . I look out of the window a moment, musing, then write on, quite unaware of the passage of time. . . . Now when I catch myself thinking, "Colleague So-and-So won't like this," I scarcely pause to answer, "The hell with him . . . I want to write it anyway." I type on, and suddenly, in what seems only a few minutes later, I become aware that it is . . . half an hour past the time I had planned to stop.
>
> In this second state—the description of which undoubtedly reveals my own bias—I am viewing myself not as object but as subject. My sentences now hinge on such verbs as *want, wish, feel,* rather than *have* and *must.*

What we want is the capacity to view ourselves as *both* subject and object. Creative consciousness lies in the dialectical process of doing both. The courageous living with this "double view" is the source of human creativity.

# Neuroses as a Failure of Personal Growth

An actualizing person does not fear mental illness, but simply sees it as a failure of personal growth. In other words, the problem is a fear of moving forward, not backward. Most of us fear becoming mentally ill in the same way we fear physical illness. This "sickness view" of mental illness develops from the fact that the family doctor is often sought as a source of help not only with sickness, but with problems of living as well. Because Sigmund Freud, the first therapist, was a medical doctor, many think that therapy requires the help of a medical specialist such as a psychiatrist. In recent years, however, there has been a growing feeling that psychotherapy or counseling has little to do with the medical model that implies that the person needing help is "sick," and that he got that way because of some traumatic event early in his childhood.

Many people have become disillusioned with this medical model because it implies that there is some altered bodily state rather than a behavior problem. This implication is especially unfortunate because it gives people an excuse for *remaining* troubled. "I can't help it . . . ," "Don't blame me, I'm neurotic . . . ," "It's my compulsion that does it" are common complaints. In other words, the medical view allows the patient to refuse personal responsibility for his own behavior.

David Shapiro (38) and Erick Erickson (10) have referred to the medical model as the "marionette concept" of psychiatry, in that it makes the patient "a passive witness of his . . . behavior and the victim of his history." Many writers, including George Albee, past president of the American Psychological Association, also have criticized it. Albee has written a paper opposing psychodiagnosis altogether. He says "diagnostic efforts tend to focus on . . . inner pathology and weakness." (2)

We return, inevitably, to the concept I stressed in Chapter One: At our institute we deal with people who are essentially well, instead of treating people who are sick. We utilize polarities, not prescriptions. And, in fact, these polarities go beyond personal application to shed some remarkable insights into the world in which we live.

In the chapter which follows, taking a cue from Albee, I present a theory of therapy which starts with actualization rather than with pathology. The value of such an approach may be its emphasis on responsibility and the *Freedom to Be* rather than on impotence and weakness as starting points for growth.

# 4

# From Actualization to Abnormality

In previous chapters I have, by implication, criticized psychiatry for taking an essentially negative approach. The entire theme of this book stresses a positive search for the ultimate mutual interdependence. Further, I would like to emphasize the validity of Abraham Maslow's theory that actualizing, rather than psychosis, may well be the ideal starting point for any journey to interdependence.

By understanding healthy behavior, we can then reason back to see how manipulative behavior, "normal" neurotic behavior, and finally psychotic behavior also may reflect actualizing efforts. By starting from "comparative wellness" and reasoning back to the pathological, rather than starting with sickness and reasoning to averageness, an exciting alternative is presented.

George Albee, past president of the American Psychological Association, had said that "The most compelling reason

## Theory

. . . for [the] persistence of the disease model has been the absence of a satisfactory alternative." (1) This chapter attempts to present such an alternative—albeit an incomplete one.

My research suggests that the "wellness" of actualizing persons begins with the ability to express themselves creatively on two basic polarities: strength-weakness and anger-love. These basic polarities are shown in Figure 3.

Maslow, in his classic research on well functioning people, found them able to express "righteous indignation" or anger, yet at the same time able to express tenderness and love. He found them very competent and strong, yet they had an acute awareness of their own personal weaknesses. These conclusions also have been verified by research on my Personal Orientation Inventory,* a test of self-actualization. On this test, actualizing persons experience themselves as being able to be angry, *and* loving, strong, *and* weak.

Abraham Maslow has said that if, operationally, intelligence is what the intelligence test measures, then self-actualization is what the POI measures. (21) Extensive research on this instrument has now shown that this inventory does statistically differentiate actualizing or fully-functioning persons from those judged to be nonself-actualizing. (41) Furthermore, this instrument shows that actualizing persons score high on Capacity for Intimate Contact (Love) *as well as* on Acceptance for Aggression (Anger). It also shows that self-actualizing persons have high scores on Self-Regard (Strength) *as well as* on Self-Acceptance (loving oneself in spite of Weaknesses). Thus, self-actualizing persons are what I have defined as Rhythmic in their orientation. That is, they are able to swing back and forth freely on the polarities of strength-weakness and anger-love.

* The POI (Personal Orientation Inventory) is available from Educational and Industrial Testing Service, San Diego, Calif.

FROM ACTUALIZATION TO ABNORMALITY

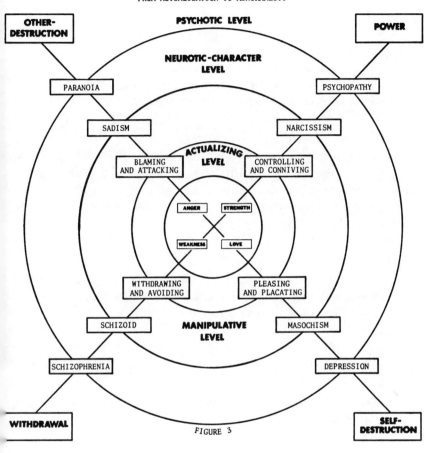

FIGURE 3

## Theory

It may be concluded that the actualizing person has a naturally rhythmic, spontaneous response to life. Like the ebb and flow of the tides and the revolving motion of the seasons, his very being reflects this natural rhythm.

But in the life of the average person, rigidification takes place. Our natural rhythmic expression is affected by parents and teachers who take control of our lives and say "yes" to some of our responses and "no" to others. They teach us to see through their eyes, to hear through their ears, to respond through their own personal fears. For an average child life becomes simplistically good and bad, right and wrong, acceptable and unacceptable. We give adults and even siblings the right to judge our worth, to determine our merit, to manipulate our love. We no longer permit ourselves Freedom to Be, we give in to the shoulds and have-tos, and our rhythm is lost. Manipulation has begun.

A study of Figure 3 shows that the actualizing polarities of strength-weakness and anger-love are distorted by the average person, who is not functioning in the inner circle of actualization. At the manipulative level, illustrated in the figure by the second circle, genuine love is replaced by pleasing and placating, genuine anger by blaming and attacking, genuine strength by controlling and conniving, and genuine weakness by withdrawing and avoiding. We now hypothesize that neurotic or psychotic patterns of behavior can be seen simply as farther steps out on these polarities.

For example, what was once genuine love, which becomes distorted into pleasing and placating, easily may lead to masochistic behavior. If one pleases and placates sufficiently, one denies one's own identity to the point of turning one's anger and hostility against oneself. Such a person allows himself to become constantly humiliated. Instead of simply denying his anger as in manipulation, he turns that anger inwardly toward himself. What is the distorted rationale for this self-destructive need? To get love and attention. Martyrdom is suffering for the sake of receiving love.

It is but a short step from masochistic behavior to the outer ring of psychotic depression. At this level the malignant symptoms of severe guilt feelings and suicidal ruminations are present. From denial of anger and turning of anger onto oneself, one finally contemplates total self-destruction. But even suicide manifests a perverse creativity inasmuch as it expresses a distorted attempt to survive in the world: "If I destroy myself, then they will appreciate me," the would-be suicide observes. Insofar as this is the case, abnormality may be seen as low-level actualizing—that is, actualizing limited to a rigid range of possibilities.

Similarly, we may hypothesize that the genuine anger of the actualizing person, which becomes distorted into blaming and attacking by the manipulating person, can easily lead to the neurotic level of sadistic behavior, where the heat of actualizing anger turns into the cold and unmoving hatred of the sadist. The sadist rigidifies his anger and delights in punishment of his supposed adversaries.

It is but a short way from sadistic anger to the ultimate expression of hostility: the paranoid psychosis. The *Diagnostic and Statistical Manual of Mental Disorders* (8) describes the paranoid as having a "constant attitude of hostility and aggression," accompanied by delusions of persecution which can then lead to homicide, the ultimate expression of hostile or other-destructive behavior. Yet even here we can see the remnants of a creative attempt to deal with the world. The paranoid, who started out by denying his need for love, ends up by directing his hatred for himself back upon the world. Because he believes the world is hostile to him, he angrily sets out to force or control the world; he comes to believe that he knows best. In this sense, his hatred may be defined as a sort of frozen love: Hitler, for example, really

*Theory*

believed that he was saving Germany by imposing his paranoid structure on the world.

When genuine strength becomes distorted, it will be noted from Figure 3, it rigidifies into what is called conniving and controlling behavior. When severely neurotic, this form of rigidity becomes narcissistic behavior. The narcissist projects an air of self-confidence, arrogance, and superiority as he attempts to impress others. When this form of behavior reaches its ultimate level, it takes the form of psychopathic or sociopathic exploitation. The subject feels most secure when his system wins over others. This is the theory of the aggressive warring nation which will be discussed in Chapter 11. Power-over or forced dependence is substituted for the mutual or interdependent strength exemplified by a fully actualizing United Nations.

Former Ambassador Henry Cabot Lodge (18) observed recently: "The world is already a better place than it would be if there were no U.N. The view of the earth from space ships and from the moon tells us, as nothing else could, that the earth's peoples are *interdependent*. We must therefore develop the will to bring a rapid growth in the effectiveness of the U.N. There is really no alternative." * There is no longer any place, Ambassador Lodge is implying, for the power-oriented sociopath in the world community.

The sociopath is so rigidly tied to his own self-enhancement that he fails to sense the inappropriateness of his own behavior. In its ultimate forms, sociopathic behavior is callous and hedonistic. It so completely lacks a sense of responsibility and an ability to rationalize behavior that its proponent ends up as a criminal. Yet even the hardened criminal often believes he is doing the "smart thing."

Finally, when genuine weakness becomes manipulative,

* Emphasis added.

*From Actualization to Abnormality*

its chief characteristics are withdrawing and avoiding. At the neurotic level this behavior pattern expresses itself as a schizoid tendency manifesting itself in coldness, aloofness, emotional detachment, and apathy. A final step leads to schizophrenic withdrawal into unreality, unpredictable disturbances in thought, regressive behavior, and a tendency to deterioration. Yet even schizophrenia has a pseudo-actualizing logic, for if one is so completely unable to cope with the world, it makes perfect sense to quit. As Harry Truman said, "If you can't stand the heat, get out of the kitchen!"

The theme of this chapter is obviously interpersonal rather than intrapersonal, for we have been focusing here on the individual in relation to others. This chapter moves away from case histories and symptomatic labels and proceeds in the direction of the payoffs to be found in interaction.

Normality and abnormality can be defined as different points on at least two basic polarities. The conceptual terminology, therefore, should include the entire range of human activity. Few theories do this. The continuum from abnormality to actualization does not purport to account for all neurotic or psychotic behavior, but it does explain much pathological behavior in terms of interpersonal actualizing. It joins functional with malfunctional theories.

In a general sense, actualization may be defined as a sense of relatedness to the world based on genuine interdependence. When, during their historic meeting at San Clemente, California, President Nixon told Japanese Premier Eisaku Sato that our two countries possessed "a natural interdependence," he was expressing this relationship in the clearest possible terms.

Psychopathology may be described as a limited or distorted attempt to actualize. When the actualizing person can feel separate and autonomous yet can let himself move rhythmically between love and anger, strength and weakness in his

## Theory

interpersonal relations, he can avoid the control and rigidification which end in neuroses and psychoses.

Perhaps we need new therapeutic methods which do not diagnose sickness but which really appreciate the creativity involved in pathological attempts to survive in the world. If, as Harvard's B. F. Skinner says, positive reinforcement is superior to negative reinforcement, we need to congratulate the client on the creativity of his attempt to actualize rather than to criticize his pathology. Perhaps therapists need to say "That was really ingenious" more often rather than saying "You are a seriously ill person in need of help."

The therapy process may be seen as a gradual replacing of the marginally creative attempts at wellness which manifest themselves in survival methods with growthful or creative activity of actualizing or expressive behavior.

Behavior, it seems, is motivated by two processes simultaneously: the need to survive and the need to actualize or grow. Survival behavior is a narrow strategic attempt to cope with a basically unlivable world. Actualizing behavior is expressive behavior which is rhythmic and relationship-enhancing. Therapy is a process which moves a person from a survival to an actualizing frame of reference, yet the therapist must appreciate the element of actualization involved in all survival behavior.

Only when we can include the actualizing frame of reference in our conceptual scheme will we be able to integrate more fully our understanding of human behavior and to press forward to the *Freedom to Be*.

# Part Two

# APPLICATIONS TO THERAPEUTIC CHANGE

# 5

# Expanding Emotional Expression

The journey of life involves a basic rhythm of living, an expanding emotional expression. In our system of polarities a person lacking the *Freedom to Be*, for example, might be located at "dead center" in an apathetic, indifferent, or feelingless state. Moving away from this dead center, as shown in Figure 4, we take the *risk* of expressing ourselves on the two polarities of anger-love and strength-weakness, in various degrees of expansion or contraction. Each of the polarities may be seen as a continuum with discreet variations —from constriction of feeling in the center to fullness of feeling as one moves outwards. Figure 4 shows certain points on each continuum with relative qualities of feeling.

The actualizing person can move rhythmically and freely on each of the basic polarities in his feeling expression. Sometimes he will move in a "maxi-swing" to points of intense feeling at the very ends of the polarities. Other times,

# EXPANDING EMOTIONAL EXPRESSION

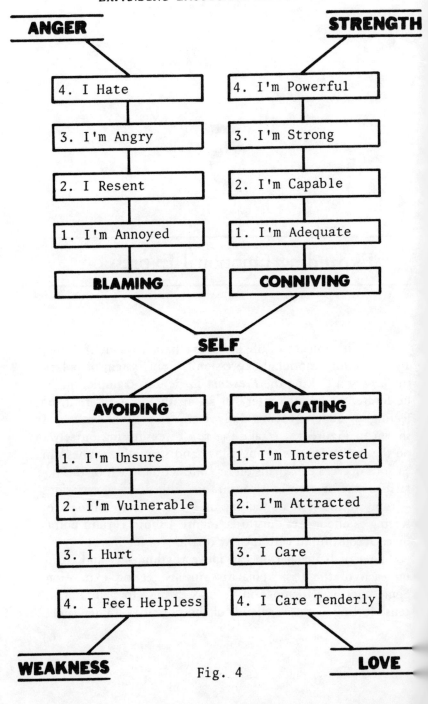

Fig. 4

## Expanding Emotional Expression

when feelings are mild or timorous, he will move in "mini-swings" near the center of the polarities. He thus has the ability freely to modulate his affect. He has developed the capacity for a "full feeling repertoire."

The importance of full feeling is illustrated by a celebrated remark of Dorothy Parker's when criticizing what she felt was a weak stage performance by Katherine Hepburn. "Miss Hepburn," she wrote, "ran the gamut of emotions from A to B." An actualizing individual runs the gamut, of course, from A to Z.

The reader may be asking at this point, why so much emphasis on the feeling dimension of life? The answer is that we have become so "head oriented" that we are not aware of the primacy of feelings in life. For example, we usually ask ourselves and others, "Why did you do this or that?" The answer, if we are honest, is "because I felt like it." Feelings do not need reasons to justify them. They are our body speaking honestly from within.

Furthermore, the question "Why" puts one on a head trip again. I try to get my people to avoid the word "Why," and instead simply ask "What," "How," "When," and "Where." This keeps us thinking and feeling and leads to more honest and productive expression.

Moving away from dead center, there are discreet dimensions of emotional expression shown in Figure 4. *Freedom to Be* means feeling the full range of feeling variations within. The reader may ask himself how many of these variations he has himself experienced and expressed recently?

Each of us needs to declare our strength in varying degrees, and it is clear that the adequate person must be able to feel and express himself behaviorally. While the "sick" person feels insecure, inadequate, and unworthy, the actualizing person feels adequate, secure, and worthwhile. The ability to verbalize feelings by such phrases as "I am adequate,"

## Applications to Therapeutic Change

"I am capable," "I am strong," or "I am powerful" represents increasing amplitude on this continuum. Herbert Otto (30) recommends the "strength bombardment" technique to help one member of a group become aware of his strengths. Each group member in turn is asked to state the ways in which he feels strong. The group then tells him how it sees his strengths and suggests ways in which he can improve them.

In addition to verbal methods of affirming strengths, certain physical exercises are helpful. These will be discussed in Chapter 6.

At the opposite end of this polarity, it is important to get in touch with one's feelings of *weakness*. In our culture there seems to be a taboo on admitting weakness, especially for men, which makes it difficult to give in to expressions of weakness. Phrases such as "I am unsure," "I am vulnerable," "I hurt," or "I feel helpless," as shown in Figure 4, represent variations on the weakness continuum. Being able to put into words both feelings of weakness and strength in varying degrees of modulation expands emotional expression and permits actualization of the full being.

The vital requirement of weakness or vulnerability as an actualizing quality is illustrated by Ralph Graves (14) in his description of Charlie Chaplin:

> He has never lost his little-boy sense of wonder . . .
> I was struck by the *vulnerability* of the most famous movie actor in the world. The vulnerability, of course, is what made the Little Tramp a figure of more than comedy. This was the greatest experience of my life. I have never been so moved by a man.*

The second basic polarity is anger-love. The anger dimension is shown in the upper left quadrant of Figure 4. Here we

* *Life*, Vol. 72, No. 15 (April 21, 1972), p. 3.

## Expanding Emotional Expression

take the risk of expressing our feelings of annoyance, resentment, anger, and sometimes even hatred. We must move out from dead center into feelings that require negative contact with other people.

Many people are afraid of this polarity, for they assume that if anger is verbalized it may result in destructive behavior. In fact, the opposite is true. The person who can give vent to "cash and carry" anger need not fear behavioral expression. On the contrary, the "nice guys" who never get angry often end up as the murderers.

It is the fear of behavioral expression of anger which causes many persons to assume that feeling expression will automatically lead to hurting or murdering someone. In reality, the expression of strong negative feeling reduces the tendency for behavioral acting out of anger. In reality, you cannot stay angry at someone if you are able to express it verbally. Expression of strong negative feeling instead leads to the homeostatic expression of its opposite, as shown in Figure 4. Thus, ability to express anger *fully* to another, more often than not leads to warm feelings toward another. This is an important communication principle.

In handling all these feelings it is important to learn to acknowledge the mild forms of each and to avoid letting deeper feelings accumulate. The experience of irritation, boredom, and annoyance at the lower levels of the anger continuum helps avoid feelings of hostility, resentment or hatred which come from an accumulation of anger.

The *love* dimension shown in the lower right quadrant is expressed verbally by such phrases as "I'm interested," "I'm attracted," "I care," and "I care tenderly." The ability to show care at various depths is a most important aspect of actualizing one's being. Tenderness, for example, is a need we all have, and yet our culture discourages its expression, as Grace Stuart (47) explains in the following passage from her *Narcissus:*

## Applications to Therapeutic Change

> It is too seldom mentioned that the baby, being quite small for quite a long time, is a handled creature, handled and held. The touch of hands on the body is one of the first and last of physical experiences and we deeply need that it be tender. We want to touch . . . and a culture that has placed a taboo on tenderness leaves us stroking our dogs and cats when we may not stroke each other. We want to be touched . . . and often we dare not say so. . . . We are starved for the laying on of hands. . . . There is no doubt that Puritanism's long restraint upon the tender touching hand did incalculable damage, as all those will know whose offered caress was in their childhood turned away. . . . [But] our best endeavors to describe an ultimate spiritual well-being say "underneath are the everlasting arms." More perhaps than we have ever realized, our physical handling of each other may make or mar the spiritual state of our civilization.

If man is going to live in a world where he can give voice to his emotions, then he must be able to modulate his affect, to feel and express himself on these two basic dimensions of emotion. The alternative seems to be some form of schizophrenia, for most schizophrenics are people who express themselves either not at all or only in extreme ways. They may withdraw to dead center and become unfeeling, emotionless, indifferent, and dead. Or they may become so extremely expressive in their feelings, so unable to slow down that they seem fragmented, impossible to relate to. The basic task for everyone is to find ways in which to express oneself more meaningfully and at what could be called normal "cruising speed" on these two basic polarities, the polarity of strength-weakness and the polarity of anger-love.

The human being needs to preserve a homeostatic balance, psychologically as well as physiologically, much as nature maintains a rhythmic biological balance. People are much concerned with ecology today because man is destroying the natural balance of life. They are also concerned with the balance within themselves. The actualizing person is one who has found an inner balance or rhythm, who can move meaningfully—with grace, if you will—on the strength-weakness and love-anger polarities. Psychotherapy or counseling is a process that helps people learn to move on these two polarities in a meaningful way. Learning to be more strong, more weak, more angry, and more loving—and to do so rhythmically—is the meaning of actualization.

Of course, this is not easy to do. To appreciate how difficult it is, we can again consider the phenomenon of manipulation, which is a distortion of actualizing behavior. Elsewhere I talk about manipulative behavior in which, instead of being strong, we are stubborn and controlling, playing the games of a conniver. Instead of being genuinely angry, we blame and attack, being hostile rather than genuinely angry. Instead of being genuinely affectionate, we often learn as children to be "nice," to protect others, to play pleasing and placating games.

Psychotherapy helps us see these inappropriate or manipulative ways of behaving. More than that, it helps us express ourselves in actualizing rather than manipulating ways. People somehow tend to get fixated on just one polarity, or to withdraw to dead center and refuse to move. They need "growing edges"—frontiers that extend into areas in which they have not been able to express themselves fully.

If you are not sure in which area you express yourself well or not so well, ask your wife or husband, sweetheart or boyfriend. They have had experience with your behavior patterns and certainly can tell you what seem to be your basic areas of unexpressed affect. I do not mean to suggest that other areas should be ignored. Basically, self-actualization re-

## Applications to Therapeutic Change

quires us to take the risk of moving into *all* the polar areas of living, feeling, and valuing.

In *The Book on the Taboo Against Knowing Who We Are,* Alan Watts (51) says that many of us live by the black-and-white game: We think of life as a series of blacks and whites, wrongs and rights, bads and goods. We feel we "should" be white but we are afraid black may win. Life then becomes a battle between the good and the bad, the rights and the wrongs. The great Chinese philosopher Lao-tse has helped us by pointing out that "It is the *concern* with right and wrong that is the sickness of the mind." Our first task is to understand that the right-wrong game, the black-versus-white game, the life-versus-death battle for survival in which many of us are engaged must be replaced by polarities of the "and" type. Not strength *versus* weakness but strength *and* weakness, not anger *versus* love but anger *and* love are required for self-actualization.

I want to suggest, too, that the roads we travel must be natural roads that follow the irregular terrain life provides for us. The mountains, rivers, and coastlines of the world are not neat and square and regular; they all vary erratically. We live in an erratic universe, and the rhythm of life has its ups and downs. Life is a process of moving up, down, and sideways in strange ways. Watts has suggested that life can be ordered, for order can be imposed on chaos just as a system of latitude and longitude can be imposed on the earth to give us the typical map we have all used and seen in atlases. A good thing to remember, though, is that the world is not *really* that way; a natural rhythm of life requires experiencing this unevenness.

In *Man's Search for Meaning,* Viktor Frankl (11) says that the role of the therapist is like that of an eye specialist as opposed to that of a painter. Whereas a painter tries to present a picture of the world as he sees it, an ophthalmologist tries to help his patient see the world *as it really is for him*. The therapist broadens his client's visual field and so helps him see a full spectrum of actions, feelings, meaning, and values. According to Frankl, our journey in life can be enhanced by doing a deed, by experiencing values or feelings, and by suffering. He talks a great deal about love as providing meaning in life, and he also talks about finding meaning in suffering. One of the basic tenets of Frankl's therapy, called *logotherapy*, is man's need to find meaning in life.

As Frankl's ophthalmologist analogy suggests, self-actualization is not an end in itself but a means—a process. We must be careful not to see self-actualization in too much of a goal-oriented way. One of the most important principles of the actualizing life is to live fully in the present. Many of us make plans for the future that we never enjoy when they mature, because by then we are living for still another future. As Alan Watts has pointed out, first we attend kindergarten to prepare for elementary school; then at elementary school we prepare for secondary school, where we prepare for college; even graduation is no fulfillment because new quotas have been established, and now we must progress from sales manager to vice president. Eventually the insurance and investment people help us plan for retirement. When we reach it, we find that our anxieties, exertions, and urgings toward the future have "left us with a weak heart, false teeth, prostate trouble, sexual impotence, fuzzy eyesight and vile digestion."(51) None of us has ever learned to live in the moment.

One of the really important principles of life is to see it not as something to move *toward* but as something to move *in*, right now, at this moment. We must learn how to live in the present, aware of the *now*, sensitive to what we are seeing, hearing, and feeling in the present. If we are going to do this, we must continually ask ourselves, "What is it I am

## Applications to Therapeutic Change

feeling?" "Am I feeling anger or love?" "Am I feeling strong or weak?" In being able to experience and express these feelings with another human being, our journey becomes an exciting process of mutual expression.

Seeing self-actualization as a *process* means something quite different from seeing it as a goal or simply as a *concept*. Maslow describes the characteristics of an actualizing person which he has derived from his research, but self-actualization as a process cannot be characterized in this way inasmuch as it consists basically of risking or experiencing the truth of one's own being in the world. It emphasizes the rhythmic swinging of our emotions as we respond to our environment.

A person is seen as actualizing or having *Freedom to Be* to the extent that he truly expresses himself. Thinking of actualization as though it were a *concept* leads to the danger of imposing "oughts" and "shoulds" upon people, whereas self-actualization as a *process* offers each of us the continual challenge to put his own feelings, thoughts, and emotions in process and, therefore, into spontaneous expression.

The paradox of the road of actualizing is that while we move forward, we also go back and around in rhythmic swings of developing growth patterns. Not in a circle or even a spiral—these forms are too "linear." Self-actualization is a multi-rhythmic flow where interdependence is *both* dependence and independence, and at the same time more than both. The Gestalt or whole of living is an interplay of opposites, a continuous, exciting adventure into new ways of expressing old patterns.

In this chapter we have defined the interplay of opposites in the rhythm of life as a process of moving on the two basic polarities of strength-weakness and anger-love. Just as the rhythm of the human heart and the rhythm of our digestive processes are in continuous interplay, so our emotional nature must flow in parallel rhythmic ways.

# 6

## Bodily Expressions of Rhythm

One day I remarked to Virginia Satir, "I've found that it takes a long time to really get to know people." Her reply was, "Yes, about five minutes!" If you are willing to try some of the exercises discussed in this chapter, I think you will agree with her. To be able to shout at someone, to be able to touch another's face, to be able to feel strength and vulnerability with another person are primary ways to develop very quickly a relationship that has real meaning. But they do require that we make contact with our bodies, that we become aware of feelings, and that we take the risk of expressing those feelings in a human relationship.

Alexander Lowen * says that in order to achieve an "open

---

* The comments of Dr. Lowen in this chapter are taken from a film produced by this writer, entitled *Lowen and Bioenergetic Therapy*, available from Psychological Films, Santa Ana, California.

## Applications to Therapeutic Change

heart," we must feel secure enough to risk disappointment and strong enough to face the fear of being alone. This requires a full identification with our own bodies. We must overcome the cultural tendency to disassociate ourselves and our egos from our bodies. This is not easily done, but the resulting health and happiness are worth the effort.

A human being needs to be understood as a body as well as an emotional entity. The relationship between the human being as a person and the human being as a body can be illustrated by an analogy with that elementary, one-celled creature, the amoeba. If stuck with a pin, the amoeba contracts. As soon as the pin is withdrawn, it expands again. But after several attacks, it expands anxiously and incompletely. Eventually, if it is repeatedly attacked, it becomes permanently contracted. It has defended itself from its environment by reducing its size.

Physically, human beings are constantly expanding and contracting. This is true of all the tissues of the body and is most easily observed in our pulse and respiration. But people themselves are always either reaching out toward the environment or withdrawing from it, in a process called *contact and withdrawal*. Emotions can be thought of as either expansive or contracting. Anger, for example, is expansive as energy flows to our muscles. Anxiety or fear is a contracting emotion in which we constrict ourselves. Sadness is also a constrictive emotion: the withdrawal seems to take place in our arms and chest. When withdrawal is permanent, the emotions become bound up in muscle contractions and the normal expansion and contraction process is stopped. This is what happens to many of us who have been hurt by the environment and by others. We tend to withdraw permanently and to contract ourselves and our bodies, rather than to find a homeostatic balance between contraction and expansion.

Maintaining a rhythm of contact and withdrawal requires

## Bodily Expressions of Rhythm

an understanding of ourselves and our bodies, of the fact that we *are* our bodies. It also requires hearing other people, touching other people, seeing other people. Such contact is not possible without an awareness of the physiological processes that make human contact possible, for contact is a bodily process as well as an emotional one.

First we must learn to breathe correctly. Breathing is the means by which we feel excitement, an identification with our body. Most of us, when we are anxious or afraid, hold our breath to some degree. Try to breathe as a baby breathes, from the diaphragm, in and around the area of the stomach. In doing the exercises that follow, concentrate on fully experiencing your breathing from the diaphragm. This can be accomplished by thinking of the diaphragm as a balloon. When you breathe *out,* push the breath out, collapsing the balloon and, therefore, the stomach. When you breathe *in,* enlarge the stomach as if it were the balloon.

The following are ways in which body expression exercises help us to develop contact with the polarities of anger-love and strength-weakness. We begin with the anger dimension. One of the easiest ways we have found to help people start to express anger is simply to have a "family argument." One person is asked to say "Yes" to another, and the other is asked to respond "No," at the same time reflecting on past experiences when he was required to do something he did not want to do. The technique is to go back and forth, "Yes," "No," gradually increasing the volume and bodily participation. The exercise puts us in touch with our anger, our wants, and our willing again. Standing up to the other person, even making a fist, increases bodily involvement. It has been suggested that the jaw is the place where repressed hostility seems to center, so we encourage people to stick out their jaws to one another in such a "fight." This also facilitates awareness of anger in our bodies.

A second way to get in touch with one's anger or hostile

## Applications to Therapeutic Change

feelings is for two participants to turn back to back and begin pushing each other, gently "fighting" each other with their buttocks. During such an exercise you easily can discover that you really do have feelings of anger. Although some people feel rather childish and foolish at first, these feelings, too, serve the purpose of the exercise, which is to help reactivate a more basic, childlike approach to our feelings.

A third way for two people to get in touch with their anger is to interlock hands and push each other. If they can find a rhythm in their pushing and allowing themselves to be pushed, they can discover the "joy" that comes from being able to communicate one's anger. It is joyful to feel one's capacity to relate rhythmically.

The opposite end of the anger dimension is the caring or love dimension. In exercises for expressing this dimension, the two participants, working together, can begin to feel their caring for one another by both saying "Yes" instead of saying "Yes" and "No." If two people say "Yes" to each other, warmly, this is one way of discovering their caring. Or, turning their backs to one another, they can rub each other's backs, this time tenderly. Each begins to feel that there is a warmth, a loving, caring feeling, that he can easily express in a physical way to another human being and receive from him.

A third caring exercise is the "facial touch." Most of us, as children, often had our parents touch us. At moments of greatest tenderness, a mother or a father would touch us on the face. One of the best ways to discover our ability to care for one another is to touch each other facially as a parent might touch a child. For example, we may say to another, "I'd like you to close your eyes now and I'm going to touch your face. I'd like you to feel that I'm your father [or mother]." Then we go through a touching and talking sequence something like this: "This is your hair, and it's very soft. This is your forehead, and beneath your forehead is one

## Bodily Expressions of Rhythm

eyebrow which comes down here and goes up there, and the other one goes up like this and down like this. And these are your eyes [touching his eyes very softly]. Your eyes are soft, delicate, wonderful. One eyelash comes out here and one eyelash comes out over here. And this is your nose, the bridge of your nose comes out to a very nice point and then goes out here toward your cheeks. Your cheeks are red and soft and beautiful. Below your cheeks are your lips. This is your upper lip, and it's soft and red and very lovely, and below your upper lip is your lower lip, and it's very nice and soft and beautiful. Below your lips is your chin, and your whole face comes down like this toward your chin and is very, very pretty." Simply to say this to another person while touching him or her often brings tears to the person being touched. This may seem a simple exercise, but if one is willing to take the risk of going through it, this physical expression of tenderness can be a very meaningful demonstration of the importance of caring in our existence.

On the weakness-strength polarity we have found that stamping one's feet firmly into the ground gives a real sense of the feeling of one's own strength, for the lower half of the body is where we get our support whereas the upper part is where we make contact. In this series of exercises we try to get in touch with our own strength. If you stamp your feet firmly into the ground until you begin to feel the muscle strain in the calves of your legs and your thighs, your feet will seem to become firmly planted in the ground, like the roots of a tree. This helps you feel our sense of strength and self-support.

A second method for feeling strength is to hold the weight of someone's head in your hands. Ask the other person to sit down or lie down and then lift the person's head. In lifting or holding that head while the other rests, you begin to feel the strength of being trusted by another.

A third technique for physically expressing strength also

## Applications to Therapeutic Change

allows one to feel the opposite, weakness. Just as holding another person's head enables the one holding the head to feel his strength, the ability to put one's head into another's hands helps one feel weakness or vulnerability. The person playing the weak role in this exercise lies on a bed, or preferably the floor, and pretends that he is a child again, perhaps only six months old, still not able to get out of his crib. The other person acts as his parent, and tries to make the "infant" feel his vulnerability, his weakness, as he lies on that floor. When the person on the floor is ready, he raises his hands, reaching for the other person and saying to him, "Will you help me?" It is important that this be a plea, not a demand. It should express great need: "I want you to help me, I need your help, will you please help me?" When this exercise is done seriously, it often brings tears to the person lying on the floor. It also brings a feeling of strength and worth to the parent figure leaning down and having the other person reach for him. In the last part of the exercise, the person on the floor reaches for the other and allows himself to be lifted up. As he is lifted off the floor, he can rest in the arms of the parent figure, rest his weight on his body. In doing this the person who has been on the floor experiences more fully than in any other exercise his weakness, vulnerability, and need. Conversely, the person who is lifting him feels great strength, capacity, and ability to cope.

I asked the author of *Betrayal of the Body* (19) to comment on this inability of people to come to feel their bodily feelings. Dr. Lowen observed:

> As a psychiatrist, I see people in trouble. Regardless of their trouble, their basic problem is their inability to enjoy life; they suffer from an incapacity to really experience pleasure. This problem is not one confined to my patients, it exists in society. Our society is not

oriented toward pleasure and enjoyment. It is basically
a society that is structured toward power and aims at
productivity that places emphasis upon material
things, as opposed to spiritual values, a society that
ignores the importance of the body and its feelings in
favor of intellectual, technological achievements. It
forces people into life situations that are compulsive in
terms of doing things, and offers them the only
alternative—fun, or compulsive play, as a relief. And so
the average individual moves between a routine job
in which he is required to produce and then a few
hours in which he is supposed or expected to be able to
release the tension that builds up during the day, and
back and forth from one tension pattern to another.

The problems to which Dr. Lowen refers often are manifested in an individual's personal relationships in the home. The home may not be the easygoing place it should be. Many mothers run their homes as if they were efficient factories. Children are supposed to fit into a pattern, just as objects fit into the processing that goes on in a plant. When the mother's work is done—that is, when she has produced what she thinks she is supposed to produce in terms of our modern image of a well-to-do home—then she can have her fun, she can become a part of the soft, flowing, natural order of things. For the most part, however, pleasure is pushed far into the background.

I asked Dr. Lowen to define pleasure.

"Pleasure is a bodily experience," he replied.

> Pleasure is a feeling of the energy flow within your own
> body. That flow, of course, has to harmonize with the
> flow outside. But when the flow of feeling in your
> body, when the easy rhythm of breathing in, breathing
> out, moving left foot, right foot, or swinging along,

> when that movement and the easy rhythm of that movement become blocked, this flow becomes painful. We block these rhythms, these natural, flowing sensations from our body to gain control. We try to gain control over ourselves just as we try to gain control over others, over nature, and over our environment, and the effect of control is to force us into rigidity, holding patterns, muscular tensions. Once a person is locked into these patterns of control and holding, his body becomes frozen in a sense, and it is this that is the basis of his inability to have pleasure. He cannot let himself go, he does not feel free within himself to be himself.

The inability to experience pleasure has always intrigued me. It is tied to the cutting off of feeling. People suppress feeling because they find it too painful to feel their imprisonment within destructive situations. Children learn this very early: Hold your breath and you don't feel anything.

At the same time, holding the breath also gives one a sense of power. When I hold my breath, I can be strong, I can resist. The problem with becoming strong through this kind of resistance costs one the interdependent ability to respond. One becomes power-oriented simply from the sense of control over oneself. One would like to have that same control over others, one would like to be able to control one's life situation, but in order to do so one must strive for ever more power.

Although pleasure may be defined as a state of excitation in the body, one also has to be able to release that excitement. Releasing the excitement is a phenomenon that Dr. Lowen calls "grounding." We have to let the excitement flow through our bodies. For example, when we let it flow through our bodies into our pelvic area, we become sexually

## Bodily Expressions of Rhythm

excited and feel sexual pleasure. When it flows through our bodies, down our legs, and into the ground, we have a pleasurable sense of contact, of being connected. If we prolong any state of excitement for too long, it becomes painful; holding a peak of pleasure sensation can be very uncomfortable. Indeed, this is so true that pleasure has been defined by more than one psychologist as the release of tension—that is, the release of excitement.

How, I have been asked, can we specifically increase our capacity for pleasure? A person's capacity for pleasure is increased, first, by getting him to breathe properly, which adds an excitement to the body, then by "grounding" him and allowing the feelings to flow through the vibrations of his legs. We then move into a deeper level of experiencing the feelings that have been suppressed by allowing the person to express those feelings.

I asked Dr. Lowen about therapeutic goals in this regard.

> The purpose of therapy is to get a person in touch with himself. We do this by putting a person in touch with his body—that is, with his feelings. It's a body trip, to use the vernacular, rather than a head trip. All other therapy is generally focused upon getting in touch with your thinking and hoping that through your thinking you will get in touch with yourself. But it is not very easy to get a person in touch with his feelings. He has been blocking these feelings out for a long time. He has held back his anger because it has been unacceptable to his parents. He has blocked off his weakness because it tends to plunge him into feelings of despair. He has cut out his fear because it immobilizes him, and in cutting out these feelings he also has cut out his love; he acts as if he has feelings but he does not let himself feel deeply.

*Applications to Therapeutic Change*

As I have pointed out earlier in this chapter, to get a person in touch with his feelings, you first have to get him breathing so that the vibrations flow. The subject then begins to express feelings, to express anger, to express and feel sadness.

Dr. Lowen explains:

> I've contrasted pleasure with power. We contrast the individual who is "head-oriented" with the individual who is in touch with his body. I have indicated that there are therapies that work from the head end. Bioenergetic Analysis works from both the head end and the body end, but with special emphasis upon the body and the experience of emotions. Not only does our society have head-oriented power as a goal, it also is basically a mass society, a society which denies the individuality of the person. A person becomes a mass individual because he does not have a choice, he does not have the right to discriminate. Advertising tells him what to buy, mass media tell him what to know, schools tell him how to respond. In other words, he becomes a mass individual, a person who is really an object and is manipulated by society.

This head-oriented mass individual is the opposite of an actualizing person.

Our concern in this volume is with the true individual who knows what he thinks, whose *Freedom to Be* is basically individualistic. To know what he thinks, the individual has to know what he feels, and to know what he feels he has to be in touch with his body. One cannot be a true individual if one is out of touch with one's body. In that instance, the individual becomes merely a thinking machine controlled by the other thinking apparatuses of our culture.

Many young people also revolt against our mass society

## Bodily Expressions of Rhythm

by joining the dropout movement. They do not want to be part of a society that denies individuality and humanity to a person. In their revolt they adopt ways that are different—they dress differently, develop habits that express their individuality. The only problem with such young people is that they have ignored the fact that really to be a fully actualizing individual, one must have feelings and must be in touch with one's body. This is not a matter of rebellion. The person who rebels is part of the very situation he rebels against, and can experience only counter-dependence rather than true independence.

The real issue is to be yourself. Only by being yourself can you be a true, and not a mass, individual. Because the rebellion of the young offers them only counter-dependence, their attempt to escape from the mass situation often leads them into the drug scene. In cutting themselves off from society, they have to find some way of feeling their physical entity. Because they cannot find that way through their bodies, they must find it through drugs. Drugs give them the illusion that they are feeling. They actually have perception, but the body is "dead." The tragedy of the hippie is that he does not feel his body, is not in touch with it.

How, the reader may well ask, are we to be in touch with our bodies? Certainly the need to be in touch with our bodies is not fulfilled in the educational system. Education is too head-oriented, cramming the child full of knowledge; for body awareness, it allows the child thirty minutes of "physical education" in which he is taught how to perform gymnastic feats. But the idea of feeling, of being in touch with your body—what I call "emotional education"—is largely ignored in the schools. The result is that children feel alienated from school. In many situations teachers need to be made aware of children, to be told, "These are real bodies, people who are either having pleasure or are in pain. When they're

## Applications to Therapeutic Change

in pain, they are not able to respond to the educational process." Teachers must be made aware of the need to bring children in contact with their bodies; some provision must be made for young children to be able to express and accept their feelings and to realize that what they feel is who they are.

If we deny children this basic truth, they lose their identity and become alienated. Either they will become submissive to the culture or will rebel against it in a do-your-own-thing manner. In no sense will they know what it is to be an actualizing person, to be a part of society in a positive way, to retain their own individual identities, to make an interdependent contribution, and by so doing perhaps become creative people.

Ideally, of course, all this should be accomplished through a "pleasure formula." But pleasure is not something that can be produced or manufactured. We cannot structure a situation and hope it will yield pleasure, because pleasure is tied into spontaneity. It arises by itself in a situation where actualizing beings flow freely through an environment that responds to their own good feelings. Pleasure is very closely related to creativity.

In our search for a fully actualized Freedom to Be, a basic problem suggests itself: Somewhere deep within ourselves, we feel that pleasure is sinful. This is not only a Puritan tradition, for it goes very far back in the Christian tradition. It reflects, somehow, the feeling that the flesh is the province of the devil, so that it is only by abstracting ourselves from the body that we get true spirituality. I believe that we now realize how disastrous the full extreme of this position is. Our true spirituality is in our body. Man is created in the image of God; therefore, his body is God's body. Alexander Lowen has said that God is grace, and a body that is endowed with grace is a body that functions like the body of God.

Certainly children are graceful in this sense, until their mothers stop them from being themselves. "You shouldn't feel this way, don't move, sit still, behave, stop yelling, stop running, stop crying." All the commands interfering with the natural functions of the child turn his body into a rigid structure. It is at this point that the human being falls from grace.

Every infant is born with grace. If the mother could be as gracious in her response to the infant as the infant is gracious in his ability to receive her love, I think we would not have many of the problems we face today in our culture. We would have a different rapport between man and nature, between man and his God.

"It's a lot to ask for," Dr. Lowen observed, "and it can be achieved only if we work for it. We have to work for it by being in touch with our bodies, by being in touch with our feelings, and by recognizing the importance of pleasure in the life of a person."

The body awareness techniques described earlier are correctives for a sick world. We live in a world in which people have lost touch with their bodies and their feelings. In order to renew contact, we need to develop a new sense of awareness of bodily feelings.

Awareness of our feelings is vital. Reichians and others have said that feelings are grounded in our muscle structure. Until we can feel our bodies and our muscles again, we cannot fully know our feelings. An increased awareness of our bodies, combined with an increased freedom of verbal expression, makes us aware of our feelings and brings us into closer contact with ourselves and others.

# 7

## Questioning Our Assumptions

According to the French novelist and essayist Antoine de Saint-Exupéry, love does not consist of "gazing into one another's eyes," but of "looking together in the same direction." This interdependent togetherness has been particularly hard to achieve in our culture because in choosing a mate we have a tendency to look not only in one another's eyes, but at various other parts of the anatomy as well.

While still in our late teens or early twenties, most of us make two crucial decisions: the direction of our life work, and our mate for (presumably) the duration of our journey. Changing either of these decisions involves two quite different sets of problems. Lou, in his relationship to Joleen, faced them both.

As we have seen, Lou—who graduated later in life than most of his classmates—had very nearly chosen a career in law, which for him would have been the wrong vocation.

## Applications to Therapeutic Change

Unhappily, Lou's decision to give up law and go into medicine affected his second major decision in his formative years: his marriage to Joleen. The initial frustrations of the first change made him unwilling to work at the necessary adjustments in the second.

"I had what you call a 'jockstrap complex,'" he admitted to me. "It really wasn't Joleen's fault. I wanted to be the best everything. If I couldn't be the best lawyer—and I wasn't sure whether I could be the best doctor—I could at least prove to myself that I was the best lover."

This attempt to assert his independence was matched by Joleen's determination to be passively dependent at all costs. Committed to letting him have his way, she would never tell him that he was hurting her emotionally as well as physically.

"As a psychiatrist," Victor M. Victoroff (50) has suggested, "I examine assumptions. The business of psychiatry is to inventory assumptions and to run a trace to their source in personal history."

Dr. Victoroff defines assumptions as ideas or principles which are held to be self-evidently, axiomatically true. He goes on to break them down into three categories:

1. Assumptions may be accepted as the result of expediency or accident.
2. Assumptions may be accepted because of slavish identification with others who are admired or hated.
3. Assumptions may be inductive summations, acknowledged springboards into the unknown, accepted on a frankly tentative basis until something better comes along.

"It is astonishing," Dr. Victoroff concludes, "how much we take for granted."

## Questioning Our Assumptions

It is indeed. As an Actualization Therapist, I believe that it is my duty not merely to list assumptions, but to *question* them. For example, both Lou and Joleen were constantly making assumptions about their problems—most of which, as it turned out, were incorrect. Lou and Joleen had selected each other out of an unconscious need fulfillment process. They simply did not know why they made the choice or how; they thought it was because of that much misused designation for interpersonal relationships, love. As we shall see, few of us really understand love in its many manifestations. The rhythm of life involves the problems of mate choice, the problems of expectations and disappointments. We must attempt to understand more fully this important life decision in terms of this rhythm.

Most of us, having failed to complete the first part of our life journey, the journey alone, at all satisfactorily, reach our late teens and early twenties riddled with self-doubts and possessing a low self-esteem. Inevitably, most of us, including Lou and Joleen, marry someone in order to get something out of him or her. As we have already seen, Lou was seeking a reaffirmation of his manhood and Joleen an escape from the uncertainties of adolescence. Each was making a false assumption on the basis of "expediency" and each was justifying that assumption by interjecting the love factor.

We tend to make expediency assumptions because we have never actualized our being to the independent stage. Never really having separated from our parents, we find it impossible to arrive at an interdependent relationship with them. (Physically removing ourselves often has little to do with our achieving independence. Indeed, the opposite might well result when, fnding ourselves living alone in an apartment for the first time, we run "home" on the slightest pretext.)

We enter the married state harboring two predominant emotions: high expectations and high fears. Lou feared that

## Applications to Therapeutic Change

he would not make a competent lawyer, transferred that fear to his internship, and ultimately feared that, in his marriage, his manhood would be threatened. Joleen had high expectations that Lou would prove her womanhood, her independence from her parents, and had those hopes dashed in the nuptial bed for reasons that she failed to understand. Each selected in the other those supposed qualities that seemed to fulfill his or her dependency needs.

We do not necessarily communicate our expectations or fears to our intended partner; we select someone in the hope that he or she will provide or supplement those qualities in ourselves that we have developed only partially or not at all. We all have heard a young bride and groom say that now their lives are "complete," without their fully understanding the psychological nuances of such a declaration.

The marriage journey, then, can be said to be a continuation of the manipulative journey in our uninterrupted orchestration of the rhythm of life. We marry with a feeling of being half-developed, hoping that we have selected a person who will bring us a sense of completeness, or wholeness. The bride may turn to the groom and say with love and sincerity, "At last, darling, we are truly *one*." To which the husband may well reply, "Yes, sweetheart, but don't forget to set the table for two."

This is the crux of the problem. A manipulative marriage based on unconscious needs leads to a false feeling of wholeness or completeness simply because two divergent parts rarely add up to an emotional whole. The relationship is basically need-oriented, with each person demanding that the other live up to expectations while fearing that the demands will not be met. What occurs is only partial fulfillment: two half-developed people marry and manage to feel some sense of wholeness—but only for a while.

How do we cope with a broken relationship? First, I have an inflexible rule that husband and wife are never a part

## Questioning Our Assumptions

of the same group. They must develop separately, both in private consultation with me or one of our staff therapists and in the group situation. This does not mean, however, that I discourage them from associating socially away from the Institute. As a matter of fact, I encourage them to date, to be with one another in social situations, and to behave as though each was discovering the other for the first time.

More practically, I get the individual with whom I am working to break through false assumptions and come to grips with what Dean Rusk, in international relations, used to refer to as "the other side." (Once again, the person-to-person, nation-to-nation parallel is clear.) Let's sit in on a group session with Lou to see some of these principles in action.

"Why not be yourself," I suggested to Lou, "and be Joleen as well. Let's see how things look from both your points of view."

Lou, facing an empty chair, addressed an imaginery Joleen —who, at that very moment in another part of the Institute, may well have been attempting the same process in reverse.

"It just hasn't worked out," Lou began. "Everything seemed fine when we started . . . when we got married. I thought it was going to last forever. But you just don't get to know someone until you're married to them. . . . Maybe . . . no, I *know* that it was partly my fault, but beginning with the sex business, I . . ." He hesitated here, moistened his lips, looked around at the group who sat watching with interest but without an outward emotion. "Well, I felt it was all wrong right from the start. I guess I should have told you . . ."

"No 'shoulds,'" I interrupted him. "Say what you feel, not what you feel you should feel."

Lou looked from me to the empty chair. His voice began to rise as he expressed his true feeling.

"Honest to Christ, Jol," he continued, "you frustrate the

## Applications to Therapeutic Change

hell out of me. I appreciate your working and all that but . . . I mean you're not even a good piece of ass. You lie there looking up at me reproachfully as though I should . . . as though I have to be grateful for all you're doing."

Lou was almost shouting now as he let it all come out. "It was a two-way deal, you know. You were going to get something out of it too. I mean, Christ, the Madonna bit drove me right out of my head. I mean, it isn't all sex, I know, but that 'long-suffering' shit spilled over into everything. It's as though you were telling me that I was taking advantage of you or something."

Lou pressed his hands to his face, very agitated now. "Jol, it just hasn't worked out," he told his imaginary mate. "You were a big girl going into this and I don't want to hurt your feelings and maybe sex triggered the whole thing . . . I don't know. All I do know is that you bore the hell out of me, you frustrate me, you make me feel guilty, and I can't stand being around you."

Lou slumped back on the couch, staring straight ahead of him, unwilling to meet anyone's gaze.

"Now," I tell him, "get up and sit in the chair. Be Joleen. Answer what you've just said."

"I can't."

"I think you can. You know her, you know what her feelings are; try to put yourself in her place. Let's hear her side of it."

Reluctantly Lou got up and sat down in the other chair. He saw that the group was participating with genuine interest. *They* wanted to hear Joleen's side of it. He looked at me and I nodded reassuringly. "Tell Lou your side," I urged.

This was a difficult but an important time for Lou. It took a great deal of courage to speak out in the way he had just done, and it would take even more to turn around and project himself into the object of his anger.

## Questioning Our Assumptions

"I . . . don't . . . think that is quite fair," he began timorously. "I really wanted to work and help us both make your career. I don't think its fair to think that I knew everything about life . . . about sex."

Lou, as Joleen, sat in the chair and stared morosely at the empty couch seat. He didn't say anything for some time; no one in the group said anything either.

"Didn't Lou expect a lot of you?" I interjected.

"He expected me to *know* everything," Lou-Joleen complained. "How could I when he . . ."

"*You*," I interrupted. "Talk to Lou directly."

". . . when you knew very well that you were the first man I'd even been with. It's . . . it's not my fault if I couldn't have an orgasm. You should . . ."

"No 'shoulds,'" I reminded Lou-Joleen.

"You didn't even try to teach me. All you were worried about was proving what a big stud you were. Maybe I was lying there looking at you reproachfully. Who wouldn't? When you started screwing—and I didn't use *that* word until I married you—around with all those pre-med whores. I don't see why I have to work so that you can prove what a big man you are."

"Now," I said quietly, "be Lou again and answer her."

He changed places more quickly this time, anxious to continue the dialogue.

"Look, Jol," he began almost before he sat down, "I'm sorry about the sex. But it's too late now. You've worked, and I appreciate it, but I can't go on thanking you forever. You're a good-looking girl and you'll have no trouble finding a nice guy." His tone was placating, almost beseeching in his attempt to justify himself. "I admit that I've made some mistakes, but I don't think we should devote the rest of our lives to paying for them. You're not happy with me now; you said so. Whether or not we have an orgasm isn't the main thing, now. It's all gone past that."

## Applications to Therapeutic Change

And so the therapeutic process continued. The repeated role exchange brought about an understanding of the other person's position. As Lou (and, in her group, Joleen) switched seats on succeeding nights, their arguments became less vitriolic as they grew to understand each other's false assumptions.

This role reversal is not sufficient in itself, of course; Lou and Joleen have a lot to overcome before they decide that the proper solution is to return to one another or to part permanently. But it is a surprisingly effective base from which to attack the problem.

How interesting it would be to project this technique onto the broad canvas of the geopolitical scene. Such experiments hav been conducted at the RAND Corporation. Suppose the United Nations split their opposing forces into just such groups with the United States in one chair facing Russia in another, while each first presented its viewpoint, then traded chairs to defend the position of the other?

I conducted one such experiment with a colleague in order to demonstrate the practicality of the hypothesis. I took the role of the United States, he of the Soviet Union.

"I don't trust you," I began. "International communism traditionally has set out to destroy our way of life. I really hate what you stand for and I'm telling you now that I'm on my guard. You try anything and I'll wipe you off the face of the earth. Don't think you're fooling anyone with peace overtures. You're spreading out all over the globe, trying to undermine our friends and bleed us to death."

"You've always tried to push east in Europe," my colleague countered. "You've encircled us with missile bases and Polaris submarines loaded with nuclear weapons. Every day your bombers fly within bombing distance of our cities. We must protect ourselves from the capitalist plot to overthrow our government and take the power away from the proletariat. You are warmongers who need war to survive. You are our enemy and we will continue to arm to avoid destruction."

"We keep bombers in the air and Polaris submarines at sea because we know that as long as they are there you won't launch any sneak attack," I replied. "You know that we can destroy you. If we didn't have that power you would overrun our allies in Europe and Asia, then launch a thermonuclear attack on us at home. We know all about those big rockets you have that put your space lab in orbit. Those rockets can carry warheads, too."

"If we hadn't had the first big rockets to put a man in orbit around the earth, you would have tried to crush us by now. Our rockets frightened you, didn't they? They kept your adventurous friends in Europe from helping the traitors in countries friendly to us from overthrowing their governments. You want to destroy us so you can exploit the small countries that we protect."

We now reversed roles much as Lou and Joleen had done.

"We are still way behind you in development," I said, now speaking for Russia. "We know that you are more powerful and rich than we are. We have been exploited for centuries by a ruling class that called themselves your friends. We see you build bases all around us and we worry about our survival. Why would you build so many nuclear weapons and point them at us if you did not plan to use them to crush our government and put your capitalist friends back in power?"

"You send out people all over the world to spy on our friends, to steal our nuclear secrets, and to start revolutions near our shores," my colleague charged. "International communism is dedicated to the overthrow of capitalism. We are sensitive to this subversive activity and must use every means possible to protect ourselves. When you put the first man in space we knew that it was as much a military development as a peaceful one. We can't have you arousing the new nations against us while your rockets overfly our country. You talk of peace but you have spies everywhere trying to cause trouble."

"Everyone uses spies. It is our only way of making sure that we know of your warlike plans. Building so many armaments to defend ourselves is keeping our nation poor. We needed the prestige of the space effort to show you that we could not be bullied by your technology. Three brave cosmonauts died, even as your brave men died because of it. If there was some way of making sure that you did not mean to destroy us we would like to cut down on this mad race. But we can't."

"It seems that we use the same words—'protect' and 'fear' and 'peace,'" my "American" colleague said. "Perhaps we should listen to one another a little more. We are both saying the same things about one another. Perhaps, without our consciously realizing it, communism and capitalism have both changed in the last fifty years. Historically everything changes in a half-century. Why not our two systems?"

"I can speak for you and you for me. I begin to feel a sense of interdependence."

"We both have a sufficient independence to cooperate with one another because we want to, not because we have to."

Having examined the rhythm of life and applied it on both a limited and large scale, we return inevitably to my quotation from Saint-Exupéry at the beginning of this chapter: "Looking together in the same direction" takes on an added meaning when it is projected on a global scale. I find

## Questioning Our Assumptions

most stimulating the possibility that what we accomplish daily on a therapeutic basis, if adopted by actualizing heads of state, might contribute to a peaceful and mutually productive international interdependence. In later chapters, we will examine more fully the political implications of our therapeutic theories.

# Part Three

# APPLICATIONS TO LIFE, LOVE, AND MARRIAGE

# 8

## Love, the Human Encounter

I have suggested that the average young couple falls in love in an attempt to fulfill unconscious needs. They select each other not because they really "love," but because they feel incomplete and the other person temporarily makes them feel whole. I would further suggest that a couple such as Lou and Joleen view marriage as a *workshop for growth,* a relationship where they can develop the incomplete portions of themselves and can relate together in an actualizing way.*

Any attempt to define an actualizing relationship in terms of a human encounter must first address itself to what is meant by "love."

In the preceding chapters I have several times redefined

---
* The dimensions of love described in this chapter are measured by the *Caring Relationship Inventory,* published by Educational and Industrial Testing Service, San Diego, California. (42)

## Applications to Life, Love, and Marriage

the role of *Actualization Therapy*. It is not my intention to point up what I believe are past mistakes in the application of psychological theory to the life experience, but rather to go forward, building on the foundations laid by such respected men as Frederick Perls and Abraham Maslow, and adapting, as any good builder must, to the changing human conditions that make alterations in the therapist's approach to his goals inevitable.

"Particularly strange," Abraham Maslow said, "is the silence of psychologists on the subject of love." And nowhere more strange, in my opinion, than in their approach to love, the most important of human experiences. Psychological and sociological textbooks practically never discuss the subject. Most ludicrously, the word "love" is often not indexed in books dealing with interpersonal relationships!

Love, it seems, lacks scientific respectability. It has a romantic, unscientific connotation that turns psychologists off. They cannot define it without resorting to poetic ambiguities, and when a psychologist cannot define something he is in much the same position as a priest grappling with heretical doctrine: he cannot relate it to his own experience, so he sniffs suspiciously at it and pretends it is not there.

In the experiential sense, love may be defined as an authentic human encounter. I define human encounter as two persons *grasping* each other in emotional contact, having genuine mutual *concern* for the welfare and fulfillment of each other. Ideally when this happens, the Lous and Joleens of the world experience each other along the four basic dimensions of *empathy, friendship, eros,* and *agape*. (In Chapter 12 we shall discuss these four levels of encounter in relation to the Universal Man.) These dimensions seem to occur almost in sequence as we relate to another human being.

1. When we first meet as a man and woman, there is always, to some extent, a feeling of *eros,* the first aspect of the

human encounter. Eros is a total feeling that is sometimes compared to sexual love, but it is much more than that. Rollo May has suggested that when a man meets a woman whose beauty attracts him, it is like seeing a bouquet of flowers. The man hopes that the woman shares his feelings—which, of course, include a sexual interest but are at the same time much more all-encompassing than that. The two erotic people—using the term in its broadest sense—experience an exciting and even creative feeling toward one another.

It is quite possible for people of the same sex to have this feeling for one another without any suggestion of homosexuality. When we meet another man or woman we may become conscious of a good feeling between us and of the possibility of a warm human relationship; here, we may tell ourselves, is a person we can enjoy and with whom we would like to spend some time.

2. After we have met another person, there often transpires an interchange that gives us the feeling that we are grasping each other, that we have known or been looking for each other for some time. This is *empathy*, the "pathos-in" to another human being; it is not to be confused with sympathy or getting involved with someone else subjectively. Empathy may best be described as a feeling between two individuals that is characterized by a real sense of caring for one another even though meeting for the first time; it is a feeling *with* rather than *for* the other.

3. Then, if two people like Lou and Joleen wish to pursue the relationship, they next reach the level of encounter called *friendship*. Friendship, derived from the Greek *philia*, here means simply that two people enjoy each other and are glad to be together. In friendship we become aware that the other person is a human being who is good for us, and we strive to affirm this sharing, this faith in the trust relationship that is developing between us.

4. *Agape,* a biblical term connoting "charity," completes

our four levels of human encounter. Agape, as I use it here, is the capacity to affirm the welfare of some other person beyond one's own; in theology the term is used to express the kind of love that God has for man. Rather than "charity," I prefer to call it a simple feeling of connection with another human being. This includes something I am sure we have all experienced: a sense of joy and fulfillment in being with another person as well as a desire to do something for him or her. In terms of love as a human encounter, agape may be described as affection or as the feeling of concern that a parent has for a child.

When all four of these dimensions are present, we have what Martin Buber has called an "I/Thou" relationship. We feel a sense of affirmation for each other that brings a new meaning to the relationship. When any of these dimensions is missing or distorted, we are more likely to have the manipulative relationship that I have described in some detail in *Man, the Manipulator*. For example, a woman may feel that a man is interested in her only sexually, that he has no real caring for her as a person—in a word, no empathy.

"You only love me for my body" has become a classic line in the light literature of the last generation; like many pithy sayings that find their way into the language, it is based on a large measure of truth. There are always some men who will treat some women simply as bodies with which to have sexual intercourse. When women think that this is happening (as Joleen did), they have a sense of being used, of being treated as things, of being prostituted. The current overreaction against this syndrome is found in the Women's Liberation Movement, whose sisters seek to deny men access to the traditional sources of pleasure as a form of protest. From what I can make out, "Women's Lib" adherents would like to be loved for their minds, too—a valid if not always attainable goal.

## Love, the Human Encounter

On the other hand, in the human encounter, we may feel that people are interested in us only in the godlike sense that they only want to save our souls. When this happens we also feel "used" because these people are trying to play God with us and care nothing about us as individuals. There appears to be no interest in any future relationship; the other person is merely manipulating us to enhance his or her godlike self-image.

The "con" man who treats us with a false empathy in order to get us in a frame of mind to do his bidding is another example of the misuse of empathy.

Finally, in some supposed friendships, we feel the putative friend is trying to use us in order to achieve his or her own ends. Here again, we generally would do well to heed our suspicions.

The absence or distortion of one or more of the four types of love just described is one way of defining a manipulation of the human encounter relationship.

If I, as your friend, use that friendship for the realization of some selfish need, then you are being manipulated. If a woman who has been married for twenty years feels her husband wants her only for sex, then she feels manipulated. Even empathy can be used manipulatively to get someone to do our bidding.

I suggest that there is a similar *four-stage caring sequence* that parallels the various periods of man's development.

1. The *eros stage* lasts from birth to six years. It is characterized by dependence and defense as the child relates to the mother in a most physical, sexual manner, both through touching her breasts and through her fondling of the child in turn.

2. The *empathy stage of life,* from six to twelve years, is characterized by the development of masculine and feminine roles and of a sense of individuality and separateness. It can

## Applications to Life, Love, and Marriage

be very exciting to observe children learning to empathize and care for others as much as they do for themselves. Erich Fromm contends that empathy usually does not develop before the age of nine, and that sometimes we ask our children to feel with us more than they are prepared to feel. In general, however, it is possible to see this empathetic feeling develop during the earlier years.

3. In the *friendship stage,* from twelve to approximately twenty-one, we can observe the emergence of intimacy and identity. Contrary to the sex-oriented thinking currently in vogue among the more permissive schools of encounter therapy, I strongly suggest that friendship is a more significant part of adolescent growth than sex, because it contributes more to the development of our identity during this crucial period. We develop our identity partly in response to the feelings that others have toward us and the feelings of worth that we receive from those relationships. As Harry Harlow says, the influence of peers is probably even more important than that of parents during the adolescent period.

I believe that teenagers often "go steady" too soon in an attempt to attain the sense of identity that comes from feeling that someone cares. In this particular I find myself in reluctant agreement with some members of the so-called turned-off generation who call for the establishment of a communal social structure. It is better to take the risk of having many friendships at this time in order to learn to feel comfortable in different human relationships. (This, of course, is quite different from advocating indiscriminate sex, or as it is euphemistically termed, free love.)

4. The final love stage of our human encounter journey, the *agape stage,* begins at about twenty-one and lasts through adulthood. It is characterized by concern for the welfare of others and by knowledge and mutual support. During the agape stage of life a mature person is able to identify with

the needs of other people, to care for them in a deeper and broader sense, to love them in the way, perhaps, that Eleanor Roosevelt and Albert Schweitzer did—that is, with an all-abiding, universal love for the people of the world.

Marriage now can be seen as a recapitulation of the individual's developmental history and of the four human encounter stages *paralleled precisely*.

1. The first stage of romance and marriage may easily be identified with the *eros* stage. The cocktail party behavior and the ritual mating that accompanies it consists simply of bodies sizing up other bodies. Early courtship is commonly associated with kissing and quarreling, depending and separating. Romantic love includes such elements as inquisitiveness, jealousy, exclusiveness, and sexual desire.

2. As relationships mature and the ability to feel deeply —to *empathize*—with another develops, a sense of compassion, appreciation, and tolerance, an understanding of the unique personality of the partner, becomes dominant.

3. The characteristic pattern now emerges as one of *friendship*. One of the most challenging tasks in our later years is to deepen one another's identity while retaining a dual intimacy. This can be accomplished by an active searching out of common interests, by doing things together, by acknowledging, in our interdependence, each other's dependencies.

4. Finally, *agape* is the helping, nurturing love characteristic of the mature person with a real caring for his or her partner. It involves above all else an appreciation of the humanness of oneself, of one's partner, and, indeed, of all human beings.

It follows, then, that each of us has two chances to develop each form of love as a human encounter: during his own development and during the development of his romantic relationships. Stages that are imperfectly learned through the

## Applications to Life, Love, and Marriage

early growth years may be more fully learned in mature, evolving relationships. "Love is better the second time around," the lyrics of a popular song of a few years back would have us believe. It is more than possible that a deprivation in the early years may help a person to love more deeply as an adult.

I have been discussing love as more than just an encounter for the mutual fulfillment of unconscious needs. What I choose to call *authentic love* is a relationship in which two people touch and hold each other, share a mutual concern, and experience each other totally through the manifestations of eros, empathy, friendship, and agape. When all of the four dimensions of love are present, we experience an actualizing relationship. When any one of them is missing or distorted, we have a manipulative encounter, as in our example of Lou and Joleen. As we have seen, eros was certainly present on Lou's part, but although she had every intention of being a full sexual partner, it was missing in Joleen. Because of her willingness to work while he went to university, she projected an empathy that he was not in an emotional position to return. I think it would be fair to say that neither experienced the friendship plateau, nor did they succeed in progressing to agape, the mature interdependent fulfillment of their actualizing relationship.

During the uncharted journey that we spoke of in Chapter 1, all of us meet many people and make many decisions as to whether relationships are to be meaningful and authentic encounters or temporary, perhaps manipulative unions. It is important that we establish some criteria, some standards by which to judge the significance of all relationships. We need some assistance in determining who our true friends are, who we want to be close to, and who we want to care for. The four stages of human encounter supply standards that can help us assess the meaningfulness of relationships and add

*Love, the Human Encounter*

immeasurably to the significance of our journey through life.

My breaking down the human encounter into four categories does not in any way imply that when we feel total love for someone who really matters to us, we are not also capable of deeply experiencing beauty, perfection, gratitude, profundity, and wisdom. When I wrote earlier in the chapter that there is nothing in life more important than love, I was referring to what Abraham Maslow called "the peak experience," the capacity to fully actualize our love journey in terms of the human encounter. Ideally, in this peak experience we no longer feel our own expectations, needs, fears, and demands. Instead, we accept the other person trustingly and experience a sense of identification with the vast spectrum of ideologies and personalities that comprise the entire human race. We move, in our complete love, from people to nations, embracing all human beings in an interdependent manner, free of any manipulative thoughts. When this happens, we achieve what might be termed an emotional orgasm. Nothing matters but being *fully there* with that one person and, by extension, of being one with the world.

# 9

## A Declaration of Marital Freedom

The Declaration of Independence, a bold and innovative document when it was adopted in 1776, can be rewritten, under the influence of the Liberation Movement, for the society of the 1970s:

> When in the course of marital events it becomes necessary for one partner to dissolve the legal bonds which have connected him with another, and to assume ... the separate and equal station to which the Laws of Nature and Nature's god entitle him, a decent respect to the opinions of mankind requires that he should declare the causes which impel him to the separation.
> We hold these truths to be self-evident, that all women and men are created equal, that they are endowed by their Creator with certain inalienable Rights, that among these are Life, Liberty and the Pursuit of Happiness.

## Applications to Life, Love, and Marriage

> That whenever any Form of Union becomes destructive of these ends it is the Right of the Individual to alter or abolish it, and to institute new Relationships. . . .

Let us call this document our *Declaration of Marital Independence* and follow it, as did our founding fathers, with a document designed to ensure the peaceful, mutually dependent interaction of peoples voluntarily coming together. At the risk of arousing the ire of the Daughters of the American Revolution (whose own daughters may well take advantage of this escalation of the struggle for equality between the sexes), I will suggest a second document titled *The Declaration of Marital Interdependence* and will begin it with a familiar preamble:

> We, the people of the United States, in order to form a more perfect union, establish justice, insure domestic tranquility . . .
> Do suggest an interdependent relationship not as an unalterable tie, but as a celebration of our individual freedoms.
> Do expect one another to respect our individual freedoms.
> Do seek a balanced relationship where strengths and weaknesses are mutually expressed.
> Do commit ourselves to this relationship for as long as we both shall love.

Pursuing the analogy, we may note that this country has survived one political divorce (from England) and one trial separation (during the Civil War) and has emerged intact as a union but increasingly beset by "family" strife. I suggest that the age of Divorce-Lib is upon us and that its coming will alleviate the situation.

## A Declaration of Marital Freedom

A long-established marriage should not be terminated for light or transient causes. But when an accumulation of differences and hardship over a lengthy period of time evinces a pattern of decay, it is fit and proper to make a *Declaration of Independence* in order to provide for the welfare of the individuals involved. A simple ceremony should suffice: "We, therefore, declare that we are free and independent persons, that we are mutually absolved from all allegiance to each other, and that the marriage is dissolved. We make this declaration with a feeling of good-will toward each other, and celebrate it as an affirmative mutual choice which will further foster our individual freedom and dignity."

Alvin Toffler in *Future Shock* (49) stresses the transitoriness of modern marriage wherein he predicts that serial or temporary marriage will be the dominant feature of family life in the future.

Despite the much condemned, and much heralded, new permissiveness in our social attitudes, the question "Are you divorced?" often carries with it a strong suggestion of opprobrium. There is a sense of implied failure and even immorality implicit in the concept of divorce, even in this supposedly enlightened age.

In the spirit of the above Declarations the question, "Are you independent?" or "Are you interdependent?" gives greater dignity and a proper perspective—to both divorce and marriage as we now know these institutions. I deliberately add the qualifying term "as we know these institutions" because the rapidly expanding divorce rate is going to force a wider acceptance of what used to be called "trial marriage," but now is nothing more than legal marriage repeated as many times as the participants find necessary. This looseness of the marital knot must soon give rise to the question of why one should bother to tie it at all.

California, as the statistics indicate, is a leader in this drive

## Applications to Life, Love, and Marriage

for a series of independent relationships leading up to "the real thing"—a truly interdependent linking of two people who are together not because the law says they have to be, but because they feel the freedom to become independent anytime they choose, yet do not exercise that freedom. By limiting the grounds for divorce to "incurable insanity" and "irreconcilable differences," the state has paved the way for a guiltless *Declaration of Marital Independence,* free from the stigma that formerly attended a dissolution of the marital union.

Some members of the establishment will accuse me of sanctioning the disintegration of the family unit as we know it and the consequent destruction of the American way of life. What I suggest, of course, is just the opposite: what we have *now* is the disruption of our familiar life-style by archaic laws and social attitudes that brand anyone a criminal who decides to take a second or third or fourth mate without dissolving a man-made union. To do so is to be guilty of bigamy, and the laws against it are based on the assumption that there is something extraterrestrial about the exchange of words that binds one human being to another in the eyes of the law. Today even the church of Rome, that last bastion of an outmoded theological concept of human relations, is being forced to admit the unreality of this view as it finds that nuns are divorcing the church at an alarming rate! Sometimes this divorce is merely a Declaration of Independence, a desire on their part to do their own thing, often while remaining loyal members of the church. But frequently the ladies enter into an interdependent relationship with a human male, achieving a newfound security in their freely chosen status.

As I point out elsewhere in this book, this era, in addition to being the rock-oriented age of Aquarius, is much more overridingly the age of Interdependence, and I propose Di-

## A Declaration of Marital Freedom

vorce-Lib is one of the age's more significant manifestations. An era of free love is upon us, whether we like it or not. How do we handle it so that the millions of young, and not so young, men and women involved find mutual contentment and trust within our system?

At our Institute we encourage troubled individuals to arrive at a state of what we call actualizing by freely admitting their weaknesses in front of their peers, then gradually realizing the strengths that are inherent in a full and honest disclosure of their attitudes toward other people.

We do not begin with the assumption that if a husband and wife are having difficulties, our task is to "straighten them out" so that they will continue living together. Quite often we find that the journey toward interdependence must be preceded by a Declaration of Independence in which husband and wife, each sitting in with a different group, arrive at the conclusion that they must take a detour on the road to full actualization. The humane laws of the state of California make it relatively easy for them to take that essential step.

This year, according to figures projected from the Statistical Abstract of the United States, there will be approximately 2,231,840 marriages in the United States and 872,000 divorces. In California the ratio of marriage to divorce drops dramatically: a projected 167,303 marriages to 120,820 divorces. Even more startling is the fact that the 1971 figure reflects an increase of 13 percent in the divorce rate and only 2 percent in the marriage rate. And these percentages, the same as those indicated for the 1969 to 1970 ratio, are undoubtedly conservative.

California, then, is rapidly approaching a one-to-one ratio of marriage to divorce (San Diego County, according to unofficial figures, already has arrived at that stage) and, as everyone knows, the Golden State tends to act as a national

## Applications to Life, Love, and Marriage

bellwether in matters dealing with interpersonal relationships.

At issue is the very structure of marriage itself. What do we think that marriage is all about in the seventies? Does one embark upon a marriage blindly in the hope that the institution itself will act as a panacea for all his or her emotional aches and pains? That is precisely what "getting married" has meant to countless generations of young men and women. Phrases leap to mind: "Two can live as cheaply as one," "He chased her until she caught him." In these phrases the entry into matrimony is seen as some kind of a game that culminates in one of the contestants having either disappeared, won, or lost.

Ideally, of course, the Declaration of Interdependence that I suggest would consist of two actualizing individuals agreeing first that they are not dependent upon one another, then agreeing further that their lack of dependency gives them the freedom to be in one another's company on a basis of mutual respect and affection. This couple can then simply "declare" their interdependence either formally in the presence of witnesses or alone, as the current phrase has it, in the privacy of their own bedrooms. They would bring an entirely new meaning to the "two consenting adults" designation utilized so extensively in attempts to reform laws governing sexual behavior.

The trend is clearly toward a liberalization of our attitudes toward marital role playing. For quite some time brides have been omitting the word "obey" from their nuptial vows, leaving "love" and "cherish" as their two principal commitments to the union. This modernization of the marriage ceremony set the tone for the new Declaration of Marital Interdependence, for in effect the bride promises to love and respect her partner fully, but within the limits of her own humanity. She pledges to accompany her spouse on a journey

## A Declaration of Marital Freedom

toward a richer, fully actualized love, a journey in which differences would be appreciated rather than minimized.

By extension, I believe that the modern bride also infers that she is not abandoning her "inalienable right" to independence and that, should the union fail to prosper, she will exercise that right with a renewed declaration. A more fitting wording of the marriage vows might have been: "We, being free and independent persons, now commit ourselves to this allegiance with all the dedication to this end that is possible within the limits of human frailty."

The key to the successful ratification by the people of this Declaration of Marital Freedom is the acknowledgment that entry into marriage must be a subjective rather than an objective effort. Every crisis, in marriage as anywhere else, provides the people involved with both a choice and an opportunity. The subjective partner, driving ahead with complete self-awareness toward a goal of full actualization, will accept the challenge of crisis and emerge from the confrontation with a deeper understanding of the other person.

Love, tempered in the crucible of marital conflict, takes on a broader, more fully realized dimension that manifests itself in true interdependence. The clients who come to me for individual or group consultation must be taught to subjectively admit their limitations. We have no objective intellectualizing; rather, we work for a visceral reaction that brings out repressed anger and fear and ultimately leads to a sense of the true independence that is a necessary step toward the completely actualized interdependent life experience.

If my Declaration of Marital Independence is accused of condoning divorce, so be it. Because of immaturity, inexperience, and loneliness, people often make mistakes in choosing a life partner. Too frequently, as the English theologian Sydney Smith has pointed out, "Marriage resem-

## Applications to Life, Love, and Marriage

bles a pair of shears, so joined that they cannot be separated; often moving in opposite directions, yet always punishing anyone who comes between them." It is time to separate the two blades of the shears so that they may go their own way if they so choose without destroying children, in-laws, or well-meaning friends who try to intervene to "save" the relationship. When those two shear blades achieve independence, each with its own cutting edge, and then decide that together they can function harmoniously, each without surrendering its own capacities, an interaction takes place that is not governed by an artificial bond but by a sense of mutual fulfillment.

"He (she) outgrew her (him)" is a particularly intriguing phrase often employed by acquaintances commenting on a recent divorce. What often happens is probably that one or both of them, resentful of a premarital dependency that has developed into a nagging irritant with which neither can live, flaunts social custom and breaks loose.

Often the way to correct the situation is to excise the basic cause of the irritant—in this case, the marriage. And the only successful way to accomplish this excision, *no matter how many times it must take place,* is to remove the sense of guilt that has heretofore been part and parcel of divorce proceedings. California, to a large extent, has succeeded in doing just that; it has given birth to the Divorce-Lib movement and has provided the atmosphere in which it can sustain itself. I am convinced that California, paradoxically, will provide us ultimately with the most stable, interdependent marriages in the nation.

This chapter, as the title indicates, presents ideas that are based on a historical document whose lofty goals give us guidance in the attainment of our individual ends. Our paraphrasing of the Declaration of Independence represents an attempt to diminish some of the evils involved in marriage and divorce as they exist in today's culture. It is an attempt to make marriage a commitment without being a duty and divorce an affirmative choice rather than an expression of failure.

I have used the Declaration of Independence and the Preamble to the Constitution to help make these points. Now, to the Four Freedoms first proposed by Franklin D. Roosevelt—freedom of speech and expression, freedom of worship, freedom from want, and freedom from fear—I would add what is to me the uniquely typical freedom that I have taken as the title of this volume: the *Freedom to Be.*

Essentially this fifth freedom is what makes our Declaration of Marital Freedom possible. It presumes that we will develop what I like to call cope-ability, the courage to be strong as well as weak. It is relatively easy to prolong a disastrous marriage by constantly retreating, by exaggerating one's own inadequacies, by taking the blame where in fact no blame exists. I urge the would-be liberated person to react strongly to an unpleasant marital situation. Rather than shy away from those who are near to you in order to avoid unpleasantness, achieve your full measure of actualization by speaking out.

It is a mistake to substitute impotence or a feeling of being hurt for anger. It is in the best interests of all concerned to make your Declaration of Independence loud and clear so that both partners can come to grips with a situation that has been aggravated by their suppressed emotions.

In a later chaper we will discuss at greater length the Freedom to Be and how it applies to your everyday living. For now it is enough to realize that your Declaration of Independence, proclaimed one or more times, may be essential to a final Declaration of Interdependence when you achieve

## Applications to Life, Love, and Marriage

an actualizing partnership in which both of you will experience the maximum enjoyment from one another, both physically and mentally. Then you will both be aware that you are interacting not because you *have to*, but because you *choose* to travel life's journey together.

# 10

## Magnificent Men

Even though each of us has grown up with certain deficiencies of need and is still to some degree survival-oriented, we can learn to become more growth-oriented, to stretch ourselves toward higher levels of expressing and affirming our own potentials. I define a growth-oriented person as one who is self-actualizing, or motivated by fuller knowledge and acceptance of his own intrinsic nature. Such a person feels that he has a "call" toward the integration and expression of his deepest self. According to Charlotte Buhler, such a person has a "directional tendency" which makes for a sense of development and growth.

For Abraham Maslow's original study, he selected from among personal acquaintances and friends, from among public and historical figures, people he thought to be either "Olympic Gold Medal Winners" or at least "growing well." Such people seem to be fulfilling themselves and doing the

## Applications to Life, Love, and Marriage

best they can with their lives. According to Maslow, they are people who are developing to the full stature of which they are capable.

This chapter is based on the hypothesis that a study of a person's heroes can help one grow toward actualization.

In this chapter I would like to introduce some "Magnificent Men" * who have achieved eminence in humanistic psychology and who, in my judgment, have developed to a high level of self-fulfillment. I asked each of them to state the central ideas which guided him in his own personal and professional growth, and I believe that the following statements provide an important set of guidelines for those of us who are striving—not to become like these people, but to become more and more ourselves, just as they have become more and more themselves. As I have written before, the only danger here is that in the study of others' values, we may become self-*concept* actualized rather than self-actualizing, that is, in the former, we may try simply to copy some picture of actualization which someone else has achieved. The latter is a *process*, not a static end, in which we become more fully *ourselves*. At the same time, magnificence or actualization is so elusive, so complex, that we must run this risk in an effort to seek to understand the lives of others who have experienced this quality of being.

The important idea is that each person who attempts this study must select his *own* actualizers and not those somebody else has selected for him. Several "heroes" should be chosen to make the study subjective enough to be meaningful and yet objective enough to be respectable. Each of the subjects on my list of actualizers in the field of humanistic psychology describes his own ideas about actualization. At the end of

---

* The expressions of the "Magnificent Men" in this chapter are from the film, *The Humanistic Revolution, Pioneers in Perspective,* produced by the author. It is available from Psychological Films, Santa Ana, California.

this chapter I will summarize what I get from them: the common characteristics of my own list of heroes. References to their major works follow each name.

*Abraham Maslow* (21, 22, 23)

The life and works of Abraham Maslow stand as a foundation for humanistic psychology. His guidance, insights, and inspiration gave meaning and direction to the work of each of the men who follow in this chapter. Their theories and ideas reflect the aspirations and concerns to which he dedicated his life.

Before Abraham Maslow, psychology consisted of either psychoanalysis or behaviorism. All the men in this chapter are leaders of the new unnoticed revolution which we call the "third force" of psychology; all have been touched by the mind of Maslow.

I began by asking Dr. Maslow about the history of the development of his concept of self-actualization:

> Well, in 1935, I came into New York City from the University of Wisconsin. I started writing a book on abnormal psychology, and the question of *normal* people came up. Without thinking of this as research, but as a private interest, I just hung around with people who seemed to me to be unusually strong or lofty. I remember "lofty" was a word I thought up then. There were such people around; I picked them out and then unofficially just hung around. Two of them were very admired teachers, and I tried to understand them. At first they were puzzling. They behaved in a way that I couldn't quite understand.
>
> I had written in my journal the descriptions of each of them, and I kept on trying to figure them out. Then one day this big, wonderful click happened. The two descriptions melted into one, and there was a theory, a generalization.

## Applications to Life, Love, and Marriage

I asked if that was a turning point.

> Well, it was no longer a hobby or a casual, personal thing. It fit in with the lecture in which Max Wertheimer introduced us to Taoism. He called it "being" and "doing." It was an extremely important lecture for me. About that time also I ran across Kurt Goldstein's *Organism,* and that fit in. There are many other elements, but these are the most important.

I asked if he was writing at this time.

> Yes. And as I worked on this abnormal psychology book, I decided to have a chapter on the *normal* personality because I figured psychotherapy ought to be *for* something. My question was where is it going, what is it all about, what is it for? I found to my amazement that there was no literature on normality, or health; nothing. I got more excited and sought out more and more individuals, tied this in with my great heroes from the past, the ones that I had loved very much—Jefferson, Lincoln, and so on—and in this way it grew.
>
> As a scientific psychologist, a laboratory man, I didn't think of it as science. Essentially this was a private thing, my private hobby, you might say. But then I talked about my private hobbies with my classes in college, and I lectured around, chatted and discussed and so on, until it slowly began to come into focus. I worked it up pretty well and let it sit.

Was that theory in his first book?

> No, that wasn't published until seven years later, partly because it didn't fit. I still wasn't emancipated from the concept of science, and psychology was a

science that I had learned out of my work with animals and with learning and conditioning. But it clicked when Werner Wolfe asked me—we had talked about it and he had a new journal—he asked me if he might publish it.

I was a little timorous because here I was going to lose my reputation, for fuzzy work and nonscientific work and so on. But I did it. Then all sorts of things kept coming in, other people, other subjects, other ideas. What it amounted to was learning to see through the eyes of lofty people.

I learned slowly to see things the way they did, to understand what motivated them, what they valued, what they didn't value, and to perceive the motivations, the emotions, the humor of the mystical experiences that they recorded. Each of these were approaches which I could then pursue in this pioneering research style. It was an innovative kind of research.

## *Gardner Murphy* (27)

Gardner Murphy was an early pioneer, a contemporary of Abraham Maslow. Here he talks about the four stages in the creative process: Immersion, Organization, Inspiration, and Evaluation.

> It seemed to us worthwhile to try a brief seven-league boots journey through the history of some phases of the human potential. It was almost universally agreed that there were four stages in all human creativity. There was *first* a love of a certain person or place or idea or symbol or tone or color. There was something from which the response to beauty and to love could be nourished forward. That—and we can still be grateful for this as a central idea—creativity doesn't spring out of dust, it springs out of life.

*Applications to Life, Love, and Marriage*

The *second* idea was that the small child "sorts" out within himself patterns of tone or color or rhythm.

The *third* idea was that when a storehouse of beloved material—colors or tones or pictures or persons—has been coordinated in a child's mind, there are periods of sudden creativity—a leap, a creative flame.

*Finally,* when the great, creative work—the *Fifth Symphony,* for example—has taken shape, there still is— as we know from the Beethoven manuscripts—a long period of working it through and making it social, of making it more than a personal message, something that others can share.

*Carl Rogers* (35, 36)

Carl Rogers, also a contemporary of Maslow in his work as a therapist, combined the role of the tough-minded scientist with that of a sensitive therapist.

I think that if I were to try to figure out what kind of contribution I've made to psychology—if I've made any—it is that I bring together two quite extremely divergent views. On the one hand, through thirty years of experience as a clinician, I really have been very close to some of the most sensitive and subjective and inner aspects of individual life. And on the other hand, I seem to always be trying to bridge the gap between clinician and scientist.

The part of me interested in science insists on trying to bring these highly subjective and very delicate, ephemeral phenomena within the realm of objective investigation. I don't know whether I've really been very successful in that yet; I do feel that it is in this realm that psychology is going to advance if it is going to advance at all. I think we've got to be much more clearly aware of what goes on in the inner lives of individuals; we have to use ingenuity that we haven't used in the past in trying to find ways of objectifying those inner phenomena and making a real science out of them.

I'm not in favor of what is often thought of as the hard-headed science of psychology—until it gets to the point where it's able to include the subjective phenomena which I feel are most important. So, then, it's this division in me between the sensitive clinician and the hard-headed scientist, and the working out of this conflict, that has been the course of my own life work.

*Rollo May* (24, 25, 26)
Rollo May, also a contemporary of Maslow, is a psychoanalyst by training who has become a humanist and an existentialist. In the following sequence he describes his changing viewpoint.

> I think that Freud made a tremendously important contribution by his enlargement of the dynamics of life. His discovery of the unconscious is really a way of saying that human beings are infinitely more powerful, more evil, more good, more creative than Victorian man, in his narrow categories, had believed. The great error of Freud was his endeavor to base this enlarged view of man on nineteenth-century biology.
>
> Now, though I greatly value this technique, as a psychoanalyst I always believed that view of man was wrong. We had to rediscover an understanding of the human being as human—the qualities that are not based upon our relationship with instinctual thought but the quality which makes man distinctively man, qualities of freedom, responsibility, will, decision, and the higher levels of consciousness. This is what the existential movement has stood for. I was an existentialist long before I ever heard of the movement.

## Applications to Life, Love, and Marriage

> It is an endeavor to take man as human, to take the qualities of responsibility and freedom as basics.
>
> I think this can be and needs to be allied with the depth insights of psychoanalysis. This is what I as a humanist—in many ways the term humanist is better than existential in this area—am devoted to doing.

### Paul Tillich (48)

Paul Tillich was the greatest theologian of his time. His book. *The Courage to Be* is perhaps the best available description of the humanistic goal for the life of man. Dr. Tillich discussed the central theme of this work with me.

> I understand *The Courage to Be* as the courage to say "yes" to life in spite of all the negative elements in human existence—in spite of man's finitude, which means his coming from nothing and going to nothing, to die. Man's guilt and fear, because he is estranged from what he truly is and what he truly ought to be, involves his anxiety about losing the meaning of his life.
>
> In spite of all of this which the man of our time experiences so deeply, it means the courage to say "yes" to life, because life has an ultimate meaning, and I will live and actualize it. It takes courage to see in the reality around us and in us something ultimately positive and meaningful and live with it, even love it. Loving life is perhaps the highest form of the courage to be.

### Frederick Perls (32, 33)

Frederick Perls was the originator of Gestalt therapy. In the paragraphs which follow, he describes the necessary steps from deadness to aliveness which must be part of the journey of every humanistically oriented man.

## Magnificent Men

A few years ago I came across a paperback book called *A Cow Can't Grow in Los Angeles*. There was a Mexican wetback who smuggled his relatives into the country and told them, "Look here, the gringos are very nice people, but there's one point that they're very touchy about. You must not let them know that they are corpses."

Now, this is exactly what I would like to demonstrate and what Gestalt therapy stands for: to make living, genuinely living, people out of those corpses. This corpse-like behavior is not restricted to the United States, of course; it's part and parcel of every modern man, especially if he lives in competition with a machine. He has to be without emotions, like a machine; he has to be reliable, and he has to be without individual wishes and intentions. The lives of those people become very boring and empty. The result is more and more dissatisfaction, more and more creation of the artificial entertainment called "fun."

They have replaced happiness with "fun." All I try to do now is find out how we have petrified into being a character playing a manipulative role, often playing a phony role without any support from our heart, without any support from our wish to be, to live, to breathe. So when we start to work on this, of course, we come first across these roles we are playing, the deadness, the desert. It's very difficult for us to realize and to accept the fact that we are dead, that we are missing out on being alive and being human again.

### *Victor Frankl* (11)

Victor Frankl, who has been quoted elsewhere in these pages, writes about a search for meaning that has had a profound effect on American humanistic psychology.

> Let's speak of happiness in general. Let's take up the American concept of pursuit of happiness. My

contention is that the very pursuit of happiness makes and accounts for failure. This is because man is primarily motivated by meaning, a striving for a reason to be happy.

Primarily, man is not concerned with anything within himself, but with something or someone outside himself. Now, once he has established such a reason to be or to become happy, I would say happiness is established as a by-product, a side effect. In other words, happiness must ensue, and that is why it need not be pursued.

But how come it cannot even be pursued? How come the pursuit of happiness is doomed to failure? This is because to the same extent that we are concerned with happiness itself—directly striving for it, making it our target, aiming at it—to the same extent we necessarily must lose sight of any reason to be happy. And therefore happiness itself must fade away. This is why, although I am very sorry, I simply must contradict a paragraph in the American Declaration of Independence because I think the pursuit of happiness is self-defeating!

## *Alan Watts* (51, 52)

Alan Watts is an important contemporary philosopher who has given man's search for identity new meaning. Here he talks about the term "unconscious" as he understands it.

It seems to me that the psychotherapist today is confronted with two sorts of problems that are really rather novel for him. To a very great degree, he is taking the place of the priest. Now, he is not just a specialist who is dealing with deviant and aberrant forms of human beings. He is becoming increasingly the guide, philosopher, and friend to people who would ordinarily be considered average and normal. In this

## Magnificent Men

position it seems to me that he is dealing very largely with the problem of man's sense of identity—that is to say, who and what the average individual feels he is. In this respect the average individual has a problem because he is confronted with what Erich Fromm has called alienation.

I asked him to define this term.

Alienation is the sense of feeling estranged from everything outside yourself, the sensation of confronting a social world and a natural world that are foreign to you, that stand against you as something to be mastered. This is a way of sensing one's existence that is peculiar to members of the Western world: to feel that I am a mind or self-enclosed in a wall or bag of skin, confronted by an external world that is not for me.

More and more the psychotherapist begins to be aware that this is a false sensation, that it is a way of feeling into which we have been tricked by our education and by our upbringing. For example, we ignore the fact that the individual and his environing world go together in the same way that two sides of a coin go together. Or that a figure and its background go together; you can't have one without the other. You are looking at me, and if you could see nothing outside the outline of my head, you would not be able to see the outline of my head either. You would see eyes and nose and mouth, but you would not see the head.

In order that there should be this outline confronting you, there must be together with it the background which is not the head alone, but the head *and* its background, if we are to see them go together. In the same way, the individual and his environment are like two poles, two aspects of one life. Ordinarily

## Applications to Life, Love, and Marriage

> we are not aware of this. One of the great tasks of psychotherapy, it seems to me, is to enable us to be aware of it, to enable the individual to feel fundamentally at home in his world. In this way he comes to have a new ground, a new dimension to what used to be called the "unconscious." It is important to make the unconscious conscious, because in the old school of psychotherapy, whether they are of Freud or of Jung, the unconscious has largely been thought of as something within us, a sort of depth. It might be a neurological depth that we are not ordinarily aware of, because we are not aware of our glands functioning, or something even deeper than neurology, an unknown dimension of an inward soul.

And how does this concept fit in with Watts's own conclusions, I asked.

> More and more it becomes clear that the unconscious is not merely something inside us, but something vastly out-reaching; that it includes all kinds of social influences on us that we are not normally aware of, all kinds of influences of the natural environment. You see, a human being derives his meaning and identity from his context, in the same way as the word in a sentence gets its meaning from its context. The one word "bark" can have different meanings in different sentences; similarly, the human being has different meanings in accordance with the context he is in. If the setting makes the man, there is a sense in which the setting *is* the man.

We will conclude this examination of our "Magnificent Men" with Dr. Maslow's summary of his thoughts about the future and his ideas for research.

## Magnificent Men

I think one thing ought to be cleared up. Speaking as a scientist and speaking to students who may be reading this, I like pioneering, I like breaking open a new field. I get bored when it gets settled, and if you have a limited notion of science, this sometimes looks unscientific.

One of the things I'd like is for people to talk as if they were about to die in twenty-four hours. Then we could see who would be free from striving, ambition, and competition, and who would get down to the bedrock of life.

What are the common characteristics of these Magnificent Men? Having known each of them, here is my list:

1. Each of them has a positive view of human nature: that man is fundamentally good rather than evil or sinful.
2. Each is creative: he has developed himself far beyond the level of the ordinary man.
3. Each is more subjective than objective: each chooses to master life rather than be moved about by life.
4. Each has experienced considerable frustration and worked through crises to get new personal meaning.
5. Each has welcomed conflict and crises rather than been overcome by them.

I believe that the ideas of these men will shine as examples for every man who is seeking to achieve his own *Freedom to Be*.

# Part Four

# APPLICATIONS TO POLITICS

# 11

## From Persons to Nations

Let us superimpose our strength-weakness and anger-love polarities on the familiar longitudinal-latitudinal polarities of a world map Mercator projection. Let us view the problems besetting our planet from a fresh perspective —from a humanistic rather than a nationalistic term of reference.

The notion that the solution of world problems might easily be reduced to the interaction of individuals is nothing new. From Ralph Waldo Emerson's "Great men are they who see . . . that thoughts rule the world," to 1940 Republican presidential candidate Wendell Willkie's "One World" concept, men of vision have sought to see the world situation in terms of the human experience.

I feel strongly that courage, compassion, caring, and assertion, if transposed from individual and group interrelationships to the more complicated (but, I believe, solvable) geo-

## Applications to Politics

political problems, will suggest a whole new actualizing experience that can be applied on a global scale.

A classic example of the application of our polarities to dynamic situations in the world today is the anger-love polarity linking the Soviet Union and the small African nation of Ghana. Ghana, since it achieved independence from Britain, has attempted to love its way into the society of sovereign states. Indeed, it probably felt that the only way it could survive would be to adopt its current official policy of nonalignment.

Put simply, nonalignment means that you don't want anybody (particularly the superpowers) mad at you. Nonaligned Ghana wanted to trade with everyone, to be assisted in its development by both East and West, and generally to present a smiling national demeanor to the rest of the world. With its populace divided into pagan, Mohammedan, and Christian faiths, Ghana was made to order for acceptance by both God-oriented and God-denying philosophies. It seemed that Ghana had it made.

Retaining her ties to her former mother-country by remaining a member of the British Commonwealth of Nations, Ghana welcomed Russian attempts to woo her away from her Western ties. During the regime of Prime Minister Kwame Nkrumah, Russians began pouring financial and technical assistance into the Ivory Coast nation. And with this material assistance came personal assistance and advice from an increasing influx of Russian technicians. Russia decided to make Ghana a showcase of communism's ability to transform an underdeveloped area into a modern atomic power. The Soviet colossus offered to build an atomic power plant at the University of Legon, situated in the town of that name not far from the capital of Accra. Prime Minister Nkrumah eagerly accepted.

Soon the entire university and the town surrounding it

were swamped with Russians working on the plant that was to bring atomic energy to Africa for the first time. It became increasingly difficult to love the stolid, unemotional white strangers—while at the same time loving the British and American business interests and educators without whom the country would have difficulty functioning. Committed to a policy of peaceful manipulation, the Ghanaians determinedly bestowed affection on communist and capitalist alike until the ordeal became too great; the Russians were asked to leave (the nearly completed atomic plant stands today, rusting in the tropical heat) and the British and Americans, understandably leery of future commitments, wondered who would be loved next and for how long.

Applying our polarity theory to this international misadventure, we would prefer that the Ghanaians not have been loaded with love (much of it forced and predicated upon national interest). The people of this newly emerging African nation would have served themselves better if they had moved along their polarity, honestly giving voice to their natural resentments. The African continent's first atomic plant might not lie empty and useless if the government had said to the Russians: "We want your help and we will accept that help gratefully, but we resent your atheism and your superior ways. We cannot pretend to enjoy communism or say that we will become communist, but if you want a trading partner and a port on the South Atlantic Ocean, we will deal with you as country to country." In short, as an interdependent, rather than as a fawningly dependent "independent" people, the Ghanaians would have been *caring* for their peace and prosperity.

And the Russians, traditionally suspicious and hostile, easily aroused to anger, stand locked in their hostility at the opposite end of our polarity. This is no unusual stance for them, but we cannot help speculating how different the situ-

## Applications to Politics

ation might have been if they had chosen to move, however tentatively, down their path toward love. Instead of packing up and pulling out when it became apparent that Ghana would not buy their political philosophy in exchange for their material aid, suppose the Russians had abandoned their obviously manipulative technique and had substituted a genuine concern for the development of the tiny nation.

The Russians would have lost none of their power; indeed, by exchanging their blind hostility to anyone opposing their ideas for a self-confident *assertion* of those ideas, they would have gained strength in the eyes of the Ghanaians and other powers as well. By stressing their willingness to apply the principle of interdependence to their role at the international bargaining table, the Socialistic Bear might have won over the African nation—if not to their ideological thinking, at least to the acknowledgment that they were a potential force for world growth. Of course, the fact that the Russians are not prepared to abandon their locked-in position of anger at the extreme of our polarity points up the basic weakness in their system: they cannot, as yet, move along to assertion. If they ever do, it may well signal a momentous actualizing change in their internal structure and, with it, a chance that the world community may move toward true interdependence and peace.

The strength-weakness polarity is basic to much of the world today, even though colonialism is supposedly ending during the last half of this century. The Seychelles are a group of idyllic, British-owned, subtropical islands in the Indian Ocean, halfway between Tahiti and the Equator. In the late nineteenth century, when the British Empire was nearing the peak of its power, the Seychelles acted as a luxurious supply depot for merchant ships and battle squadrons making the long voyage through the Mediterranean and down through the Suez Canal and the Red Sea to trade with

*From Persons to Nations*

Africa and India. The islands depended upon the mother country for their very survival. They manipulated the might of the Empire to assure their continued existence. They wallowed in weakness to ensure what was then a privileged status and a superior standard of living.

Today retired English military officers and politicians often settle in the Seychelles, protected by laws that make it very difficult for people of other nations to stay there for any length of time. But times have changed. With the introduction of the jet age, the tiny islands, with their delightful climate and pleasant topography, have something to offer on their own. They can become a self-actualizing force by moving along their polarity toward the strength of the mother country until they simultaneously achieve *compassion* for the lowered status of the once great Empire and release themselves from the need to manipulate in order to survive. Again and again, we find that when people realize that they no longer need to lean on their weakness, the result is an actualizing relationship that leads to a "healthy" interdependence.

Britain, traditionally power-oriented over the decades of her world leadership, truly has become stuck on strength. Conscious that the sun never set on her outposts of empire, she considered the Seychelles as hers by right—every bit as much as an unthinking parent exercises a manipulative hold over a weak offspring. Today, in the policy of world-disengagement being followed by the British government, we see a dramatic demonstration of our theory of flexible polarities being carried out on a worldwide scale. For even as this is being written, Great Britain *is* abandoning her inflexible position on the tip of our strength polarity. In a classic display of the effect of the Tertium Quid on international as well as interpersonal relationships, she is moving cautiously, albeit steadily, down the strength-weakness polarity and is

## Applications to Politics

even now achieving a genuine *courage* to face her new world role and to abandon her once fiercely defended independence in favor of a new actualizing interdependence with former colonies such as the Seychelles. The result of this uniquely growth-oriented experience is, quite simply, survival.

Frederick Perls perceived the dangers of a static society but did not propose a viable escape route. In *Gestalt Therapy Verbatim*(33), he wrote:

> Every individual, every plant, every animal has only one inborn goal—to actualize itself as it is. A rose is a rose is a rose. A rose is not intent to actualize itself as a kangaroo. An elephant is not intent to actualize itself as a bird. In nature—except for the human being—constitution, and healthiness, potential, growth, is all one unified *something*.
>
> The same applies to the multi-organism, or society, which consists of many people. A state, a society, consists of many thousands of cells which have to be organized either by external control or inner control, and each society tends to actualize itself as this or that specific society. The Russian society actualizes itself as what it is, the American society, the German society, the Congo tribes—they all actualize themselves, they change. And there is always a law of history: *Any Society that has outstretched itself and has lost its ability to survive, disappears.*

I believe not only that the Tertium Quid as applied to the polarity theory will enable both the individual and his society to survive through the application of the growth-oriented principles of courage, compassion, caring, and assertion, but also that *it is inevitable that it do so*. Nothing could be more illustrative of the potentially damaging results of a rigid application of the strength-weakness polarity

*From Persons to Nations*

than the case of Cuba's Fidel Castro who, as perhaps no other national leader in history, has made weakness an instrument of political survival. He is without peer as a manipulator, not only of his own people, but of the great powers as well. "Look at us," he screams to millions of attentive Cubans, "we are helpless before the Yankee giant. You must do without meat because we are so weak!" Then turning around to face the outside world, he says to the Russians: "You are the champion of the oppressed classes. We are being oppressed by the United States. You must help us because we are so weak!"

Castro has achieved the supreme double-manipulation of first making his country weak to complement his own uncertainties, then turning around and using that weakness to manipulate one foreign power against the other. He lacks the ability to relate to those around him, to understand the needs and the aspirations both of his neighbor to the north and of his reluctant, one-million-dollar-per-day benefactor across the seas. He permits the Russians to build a nuclear submarine servicing base at Cienfuegos and hints, at the same time, of a desire to ease Cuban-American tensions by rescinding that permission. He caters to the Russians but, aware that nothing would save him if the Americans decided on his destruction, he keeps a door open to the north. Without really knowing it himself, the Cuban leader is moving ever so slightly and is beginning to realize that his weakness polarity leads to personal and national suffocation. He began with independence—his defiance of the United States—then reversed to almost absolute dependence on the Soviet Union. Now he is playing one power against the other in an apparent attempt to establish a kind of interdependence in which all three principals will acknowledge one another's political and national interests. In terms of our Tertium Quid, it is possible that Castro, perhaps unwittingly, is edging toward a compassion (however odd that term may

## Applications to Politics

sound in this context) that will result in a normalizing of the Caribbean power vacuum and an easing of yet another sphere of world tension.

The United States, on the other hand, gives some indication that it is not irreconcilably stuck on strength. Exercising a statesmanlike restraint in its dealings with the provocative, mercurial Cuban leader, Washington is demonstrating that, far from being entrenched in the manipulative, unyielding strength polarity that Russia has exhibited to so many small, weak countries, it has the genuine courage—a courage founded on real rather than imagined superiority—to view the strength-weakness polarity as something less than a limited access highway from which one may not wander.

It is this Tertium Quid statesmanship, I believe, that will enable our nation successfully to adapt without resigning any of our sovereign rights. By the courage of our actions, we can encourage other nations, great and small, to review their polar relationships.

The situation in the Union of South Africa is, of course, most unfortunate. Nowhere, I believe, is the doctrine of fixed polarities more graphically displayed in a love-anger confrontation—and nowhere do the problems thus produced seem more hopeless. The blacks, locked on their love polarity as a necessary means of survival, manipulate the white minority and seem far away from caring. The whites, aware of their numerical inferiority and fearful of a black usurpation of their position and of an eventual uprising, move not one inch from their anger polarity down the road toward assertion.

It is precisely because of the closeness, the interpersonality, of the South African situation that each polarity finds it difficult to back off and observe the other's position objectively. Although some progress has been made—the government in Pretoria recently announced the setting up of the first black state within the union, destined at some future time to govern itself—this seeming concession was tokenistic at best. The whites maintain an armed stance that easily lapses into fear-inspired hostility as the minority government declares the blacks to be ungrateful for everything that is supposedly being done for them.

The blacks, on the other hand, exude obeisance and feigned gratitude as they cling helplessly to the manipulation implicit in their love polarity. If the two poles do not soon begin to recognize the need for interdependence, I fear that one side or the other will resort to violence as a solution to its problems. Tragically, they will be shooting at one another from the distance of their polarities, never venturing close enough to one another to cast aside the manipulative processes and begin to move down a mutual growth-oriented path to common statehood.

From stiflingly close love-anger polarities of the South African problem, we broaden our perspective to take in two continents and examine how the strength-weakness polarities apply to a constantly enlarging threat to world stability.

China is a vast, polyglot country with complex internal problems. She fears her more highly industrialized, better armed neighbor to the north and compensates for her general feeling of inferiority in the world community by constantly proclaiming her strength. Few nations in the world today are so locked on the strength manipulation as is communist China. Almost daily we read the pronouncements of Chairman Mao telling the uncounted millions of Chinese how their dedication to work and their devotion to their homeland will overcome the threats of the myriad external enemies that supposedly threaten the descendants of ancient Cathay.

In spite of all this preoccupation with foreign enemies, the Chinese leaders know that the natives are restless. Tradi-

## Applications to Politics

tionally China has turned north for conquest; but now, with her more than seven hundred million people—nearly one-fourth of the world's population—demanding increasing displays of strength to encourage their further sacrifices in the national interest, the Chinese communist leaders must search for an enemy in an opposite direction that they can intimidate with little fear of having their position jeopardized.

Even a cursory glance at the world map shows that Australia, whose population of just over thirteen million occupies nearly as much land as China, is a natural target. Although Australians are a courageous and determined people, they are spread too thinly to defend their homeland from a determined invader. Depending originally on the might of Britain to keep would-be conquerors from her door, during the Second World War the country "down under" looked to the Americans to turn back the then strength-oriented Japanese.* Now Australia, of necessity a weakness polarity in the global scheme of things, feels the burden of the multi-million people Asiatic nation pressing down on it from across the natural stepping stones of the Malaysian and East Indian archipelagoes, already heavily populated by Chinese merchants with traditionally strong ties to their motherland.

Meanwhile Australia, seeking to protect the "purity" of her population by a highly manipulative immigration policy ("We are weak as it is; how can we weaken ourselves further by allowing *anybody* in?" their government seems to ask), must move along the road toward compassion if she is to survive. Compassion, as I wrote in an earlier chapter, permits

---

\* Incidentally, since defeat has moved the Japanese away from their strength polarity and forced them to have the courage to admit their erroneous manipulations, they have become a respected, prosperous nation giving aid to underdeveloped areas in a working showcase display of interdependence.

us to relate to those around us without having to manipulate them. In my opinion, this state of mind would be highly desirable for the land-rich, population-poor citizens of Australia.

The Chinese, on the other hand, must move away from the declared strength polarity. They must join the world community and deal with other nations in a mature, fully actualizing manner. They have already indicated their awareness of this necessity—following our Tertium Quid philosophy in an instinctive, rather than consciously knowledgable way—by joining the United Nations and allowing President Nixon's visit.

With regard to Viet Nam, it appears that the United States, Russia, and China have all been "stuck on strength" and have all played topdog games with underdogs, North and South Viet Nam. All three giants have attempted to provide the strength of military equipment and personnel for the underdogs to fight their ideological struggles on the battlefield.

All three have played the military *containment game,* while playing power politics at the conference table. At Paris, for example, both the United States and Viet Nam have come to the "peace" table with structured strategy, determined back home and by allies, and with no attempt at spontaneous encounter.

I believe that the Nixon-Chou approach in Peking represented a new era of international diplomacy. Nixon approached China with some predetermined agenda, but the flavor of the encounter was a free exchange of views without attempting to change the other. Listening and understanding, admission of weaknesses and mistakes in the past, exchange in sharing of strengths and mutual goals for the future, represented an *expressive* rather than a *repressive* and controlling interchange.

## Applications to Politics

Hopefully, the *encounter approach* to diplomacy rather than the *power politics* approach, represents a new dimension of dynamic diplomacy.

I sincerely believe that Humanistic Psychology is developing an interpersonal psychology of *peace* which can replace *war* as a means of international survival as well as of growth.

Man can experience the polarities of anger-love and strength-weakness at the interpersonal level and keep these feelings from developing into *hostility*. I hypothesize that when anger-love and strength-weakness are not expressed and permitted, then they become repressed and rigidified into a generalized hostility. When hostility accumulates or is repressed sufficiently, then it is projected onto "enemies" and develops into group vs. group war!

But expression through individual and group processes can supplant war as a means for resolving interpersonal as well as international tensions. This requires that man is willing to risk the expression of his full range of feelings in the safe emergency of interpersonal encounter.

Polite diplomatic talk needs to be replaced with diplomatic encounter in which honesty of expression is primary. There can be no walking out or no threat of destruction, but rather *expression* as the basic criterion. Many details would need working out, but it seems to me there is no alternative if man is to survive.

Propounding any radically new theory such as I have outlined in this chapter quite often lays one open to the charge of oversimplification. How can anyone suggest so simple a solution to the world's complicated problems? The answer, of course, is that I cannot.

Any theory, first stated, is best stated simply. A point might be made that any philosophical or psychological premise that cannot be reduced to fairly elemental terms is somewhat suspect. Applying the Tertium Quid to nations must

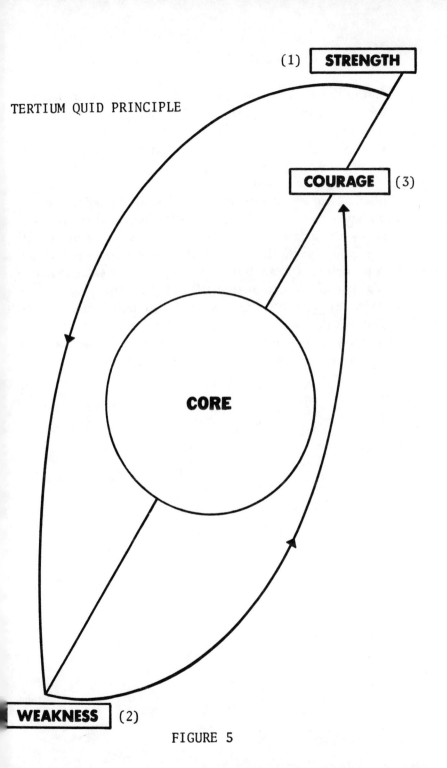

FIGURE 5

## Applications to Politics

naturally take into account the painstaking, often lengthy therapeutic process described in Chapter 2. My successful attempt to get Lou to move from the strength to weakness polarity should be projected as we see in Figure 5, on a global scale.

A nation, or person, stuck on strength must first make the often agonizing journey all the way across the polarity to the weakness condition. We must first be prepared to bare ourselves completely, to "em-bare-ass" ourselves, as I like to tell our groups at the Institute, to show our weakness unashamedly, before we can begin to move from even a tentative position of reduced strength (1) through the weakness polarity (2) then, finally, back to the strength-weakness integration (3) as exemplified by *courage*. It is often a demanding, stop-and-start journey, but one that is absolutely necessary if we are to become actualizing individuals.

# 12

## Universal Man

It becomes readily apparent that broad expanses of ocean no longer permit us the independence that was a luxury indulged in by our forefathers. It becomes obvious to even the most dedicated isolationist that, in order to survive, the world needs a value system of universal dimensions, an Actualizing United Nations guided by men whose universality of spirit goes to the very heart of our interdependence goals.

Who are these "Universal Men"? Former Republican presidential candidate Wendell Willkie again comes to mind, as does Democratic presidential candidate Adlai Stevenson. Each had the misfortune to run against popular nation symbols—Willkie against Roosevelt and Stevenson against Eisenhower. But Willkie's declared One World policy and Stevenson's devotion to the work of the United Nations show that

## Applications to Politics

these two crossed political boundaries before their time in their pursuit of world peace.

Perhaps now, as this book is written, we have arrived at a time when a Universal Man powerful enough to implement an actualization plan domestically and internationally can make his presence felt. Speaking of the peace that he hoped to leave as his legacy to this country, Richard Nixon has said: "To build this . . . peace, we must join together in building our societies—in raising a great cathedral of the spirit, which celebrates the infinite possibilities of man himself."

In the light of what I have outlined thus far in this volume, we can now get a pretty clear picture of those possibilities and of the barriers that stand in the way of their realization.

A nonactualizing person may be said to be "dead"—because of his fear of contact with other people he shrinks into himself and takes refuge in rigid manipulative rituals that make him apathetic, feelingless, and empty. His approach to others, as I have pointed out in *Man, the Manipulator,* is to play it cool, with little or no commitment or involvement to those around him. He appears indifferent or bored, lacks identity, and is generally in a state of suspension. In the jargon of the day, he is "turned off" toward society. We all have encountered this specimen countless times in every strata of society. More recently, however, he is hiding his inadequacies and self-doubts behind a studiedly indolent life-style.

The actualizing person, on the other hand, is "turned on." He has burst out of his manipulative rituals into a willingly expressed aliveness. He is constantly driving and reaching out, moving, in his journey within himself, toward a state of interdependence in the outer world. He has what Rollo May (25) calls "intentionality"—an attitude or structure that gives direction and meaning to his experience. The true actualizer is not just objectively on a trip through life; he subjectively feels himself making the trip. Taking a "trip" has assumed unfortunate connotations in our drug-oriented society, but nothing better illustrates the feeling of totality implicit in actualization than going on a trip using only one's own natural powers—instead of the illusory self-realization brought on by a drug-induced experience. The actualizer feels a power and potential that an artificial tripper can never achieve.

Our Universal Man experiences his identity in moment-to-moment action, in the process of "I conceive—I can—I will," and finally, "I am." He feels himself stretching his potential on two interpersonal polarities of being: (strength-weakness) and (love-anger). Both polarities imply that a person is reaching out, seeking to affect others, giving of himself so that he, in turn, may be affected. Instead of trying to manipulate others through power ploys or passive seduction, the actualizer opens himself affectively—that is, emotionally—and makes contact with others. He relates to other people *totally*—with the heat of his anger, the warmth of his love, the firmness of his strength, and the gentleness of his weakness.

Manipulation, by its very nature, is implosive and constricts any expression of the polarities while keeping one empty and centerless. Actualizing, however, is explosive: it ignites the expression of polarities and provides man with a *center* of optimal functioning. This center becomes the assimilator that converts experience into self-identity; it is the living nucleus that unites the polarities of strength, weakness, love, and anger into an integrated whole and gives a feeling of individuality and substance.

Imagine, if you will, the front and rear wheels of a motorcycle detaching themselves from the frame that holds them apart and rolling toward one another until the outer treads

## Applications to Politics

of their tires touch and revolve together. Each wheel has its own center of independence, its own axis, but each now acts upon the other in a true interdependence of motion without sacrificing its own identity.

So the Universal Man—a president or prime minister or king (or you or I)—sure of his journey from dependence through independence to interdependence, is ready to experience actualizing, the interaction of one person or of one people with another similarly motivated unit to begin a peaceful, fulfilling, intertwined journey through the life experience.

But how does the Universal Man begin? The first stage of his life is the dependence stage. As an infant he must depend on others for sustenance and care. As he matures, he moves on to the independence stage. In the normal course of events, he is able to free himself of his dependence on others and to make his way in the world by himself. Some individuals, of course, take longer to achieve this second stage, and some never reach it at all. If all goes well, however, he finally reaches the fully actualizing level I refer to as the interdependent stage. Now—and this is important—he does not *need* to be *either* dependent or independent and is free to choose to be either or both.

The Universal Man can *choose* to relate to other human beings, *choose* to have relationships and yet not need those relationships in the sense of being dependent on them. He can *choose* to withdraw and be independent; he can *choose* to make contact (as in our motorcycle example) and be dependent while permitting others to be dependent on him.

An actualizing relationship includes all three stages interacting simultaneously, as illustrated in Figure 6. This secular "blessed trinity" is based on mutual dependence, the basic difference between this and simple dependence being that the dependence one finds in an actualizing relationship comes

# AN ACTUALIZING RELATIONSHIP IN TERMS OF THE ACTUALIZING "TRINITY"

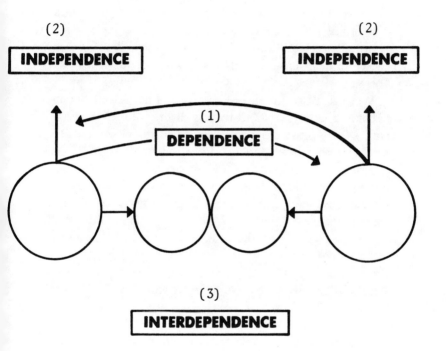

FIGURE 6

## Applications to Politics

about through choice rather than compulsion. As the arrows in our simple drawing indicate, two people (or nations) may proceed alone on a vertical course, then make an independent decision to proceed together on the horizontal plane. Each has developed sufficient maturity so that he does not need the other, but instead freely decides to assume a nondependent interdependence. Thus the two become interdependently related out of a sense of freedom, a sense of choice, and a sense of well-being toward the other party involved.

Well, it all seems simple enough! The person destined to become a Universal Man travels through his three stages, becomes fully actualized, and goes on to fulfill his destiny. The very fact that he is highly motivated at the outset seems to guarantee a safe journey toward actualization. Interestingly enough, however, the person who eventually achieves the most satisfactory actualization is the one who very often needs guidance at our Institute. Usually a sensitive individual, the nonactualizer tends to be intensely aware of his or her potential shortcomings and resists growth for that very reason.

Abraham Maslow (21) was among the first to catalog the three basic reasons why we shy away from our journey toward actualization. First, we have the *Jonah Complex* in which the individual decides that it is too dangerous to be great, so he runs from his fate just as Jonah tried in vain to flee from his destiny. This individual deliberately plans to be less than the best he is capable of becoming and evades the reality of his own capacity. An actualizing person, one made aware that he is a victim of this complex, is in constant search for his mission or call in life.

Another problem is *Countervaluing*. In this case the individual tends to countervalue greatness in others. He scoffs at the greatness of the Universal Man because it makes him feel less worthless for not having achieved it himself. By contrast, the actualizing person learns to admire and appreciate greatness in others. He learns from them and strives to emulate them.

The third trap is the *Fear of Paranoia,* which induces the subject to fear that others will consider him paranoid or arrogant if he openly professes his ambitions. By adopting a posture of mock humility or pseudo-stupidity, he manipulates his potential tormentors.

# The Four Levels of Encounter

The actualizing relationship can be examined in terms of eros, empathy, friendship, and agape—the four levels of encounter. Eros is that stage of growth that we first experience as children (or in an emerging nation). We relate to one another as individuals by touching or other erotic means; a small, new nation is often referred to as "feeling its way" in the strange world of geopolitics and "trying to get the sense" of its position in relation to the world powers.

As a person or nation moves into its preadolescent stage, a sense of closeness of empathy begins to form, creating an awareness of a relationship to those around him. With adolescence comes friendship, a willingness to accept a mutual affinity until, in adulthood, we begin to feel agape, or a godlike caring for one another.

An actualizing relationship requires the power and tenderness of eros, the understanding and vulnerability of empathy, the assertiveness and relatedness of friendship, and the responsibility and receptivity of agape. The degree to which any one of the four levels is absent or distorted decreases the actualizing nature of that relationship. When only one is present—as in the sexual relationship between Lou and Joleen, for example—then the interaction is very limited.

## Applications to Politics

To sum up, an actualizing relationship needs appreciation and individuality as well as differences in both parties. Appreciation provides a foundation, an ability to appreciate the uniqueness of one's partner so that the two of you feel a sense of substance in your togetherness. Individuality provides interest; the mere fact of individuality presupposes a sense of identity which gives each party something to care for. Difference allows for growth; growth can only take place when two people or national groupings, fully appreciating each other's differences, begin to actualize together.

The Universal Man has experienced the four levels of encounter and, in so doing, has arrived at the fully actualized state of interdependence that enables him to enjoy a complete life experience. His interdependence is a living testament to the development of his fullest human potential. It is my belief that he will use this potential to finally bring about the "peace in our time" that British Prime Minister Neville Chamberlain mistakenly predicted just before the outbreak of the Second World War.

Chamberlain, a good example of a nonactualizing individual, went to talk with Adolph Hitler not as the representative of a fully actualized nation prepared to seek true interdependence with Nazi Germany, but as someone still uncertainly feeling his way through the dependence stage, unsure of his position and afraid to meet the Germans as an autonomous agent. Chamberlain was in Munich not because he wanted to treat with Hitler as an actualized equal, but because he wallowed in weakness and feared the Nazi colossus. The result was a holocaust that took the lives of millions of people. Who can say what would have happened if, instead of coming home with a spurious peace treaty, the Prime Minister had approached the German leader from a position of true interdependence, a position of strength from which he chose to discuss a mutually dependent relationship?

## Universal Man

Contrast the behavior of our own chief executive when he boldly lowered trade restrictions with mainland China. An unthinkable, even traitorous act twelve months earlier, this suggestion of a *détente* with a former implacable foe was hailed around the world by other Universal Men as a triumph of enlightened internationalism. One could never imagine the earlier Nixon, the dogged pursuer of Alger Hiss—the dependent Nixon—initiating such a profound change in policy, much less traveling 12,000 miles to chat with Mao Tse-Tung. But a Universal Man is capable of suggesting mutual dependence precisely because we, as a nation, do not *need* that dependence—just as you too, by achieving interdependence, can escape the rigidity of your own polarities and enjoy a full realization of your potential.

# 13

## Dynamic Diplomacy

I believe that both in our private lives and in our national posture at home and abroad we are the victims of a malady that I choose to call *groupitis*.

All the way from "group grope," that ultimate expression of youthful togetherness, to the interplay of the big powers on the rapidly changing global scene, we tend to express ourselves in terms of complete units or groups. My son tells me that my generation will never understand his. He sees me as part of a group and himself as part of a group rather than each of us a unit that, with other units, forms a group.

In the United Nations "we" the Americans watch "them" the mainland Chinese to see how "they" will react to "our" dealings with the Russians. With few exceptions, we do not think of the leaders of other countries as individual personalities; rather, we see them as reflections of that great amorphous body comprising the people they represent.

## Applications to Politics

How do we break free of this group-versus-group pattern? I was able to do it on a personal basis by showing my son that he and I were each made up of a series of *individual* thoughts, attitudes, and prejudices that, if seen through mutual understanding as part of the Gestalt (whole), could break free of the stereotypic control that this *groupitis* suggests. This control is a form of manipulation practiced unconsciously by individuals and world leaders alike. To hate "them," or fear "them," or distrust "them" is an easy rationalization of a difficult situation. By casting "them" (whoever they are) in a collective role, we force them to retaliate by venting their disproval of "us," thereby compounding whatever misunderstanding exists—and, in this day of nuclear weapons, bringing grave danger to everyone on earth.

*Stereotypic control*—the casting of nations or individuals in the form of indefinable wholes—is a convenient substitute for thinking. No individual or nation can achieve Freedom to Be so long as the *groupitis* of stereotypic control is practiced.

It is one thing, of course, for me to be able to arrive at an understanding with my son and quite another to demonstrate my theory on a plane that will be immediately apparent to the reader. Happily for the validity of my theory, this has been done and is being done daily through practice of what I like to call *Dynamic Diplomacy*.

First, let me issue a disclaimer for those of you who may feel that my use of political analogy somehow corrupts my theory. I am talking about the interaction of *people*, and man is a political animal. Whether he casts his vote for the president of the local Kiwanis or throws a brick through a foreign embassy window in the Middle East, he is declaring himself a part of the environment in which he exists. And in matters of politics today, President Nixon (to once again borrow the jargon of my son's generation) is a public example of "where it's at."

## Dynamic Diplomacy

It often has appeared to the eye of many critical observers that President Nixon has been simply a puppet manipulated by the minds of many advisors and that he has no creative ability to act spontaneously in the moment. But just as a great quarterback may choose to run with the ball when the coach has called for a pass, so history has demonstrated that Nixon has the ability to run the team as both coach and player. *Life* writer Hugh Sidey's (44) description of Nixon at Camp David just before the imposition of the wage-price freeze in 1971 illustrates this point:

> He had heard them all out now and spoke with the force of someone whose mind was made up. He summarized the different arguments and though the ghosts of old disagreements arose, they were not allowed to intrude. Individual suggestions from critics and friends alike had not seemed right by themselves, he said. It was only now that it all seemed to fit together. Each action was needed to fit into a whole. Nixon stepped out of the wreckage of his old economic theology without so much as a glance back. The program he sketched had everyone's endorsement. "We were like the blind men," thought one fellow there. "When we took off our blindfolds and saw the whole animal, we were enthusiastic." *

Viet Nam is another game Nixon has been called upon to coach, after many others, both Republican and Democrat, have failed. He chose to win the game by carefully losing well. There was a wisdom in this policy which few understand deeply: that whenever you win, you lose, and whenever you lose, you win. A person who can express this principle in action truly has an understanding of the deepest meaning of interdependence.

* *Life*, August 27, 1971, pp. 20–21.

## Applications to Politics

Surely no one who watched the caucus of free world countries that led to the devaluation of the dollar and cast the United States in an entirely new role on the world scene can doubt but that the President's decisions directly affected hundreds of millions of people of every ethnic origin and creed. Once this obvious truth had been accepted, people immediately began to wonder how the President had frontally attacked the historic monetary balance struck by the common agreement of the international community.

From the time of Hammurabi, the practice of *Dynamic Diplomacy* has required forceful decisions by a single individual carrying out a policy that he feels best serve the interests of those whom he governs. Historically, two elements dilute the capacity of a leader to practice such diplomacy: the loss of absolute rule, requiring the leader to consult before acting, and the improvement of communications. As a result of these developments the unit became the group, and the group was able to communicate with other groups without having to be in their presence. Gradually the leader, who typified the people of his world and was a visible representative of it, gave way to a council or parliament or congress who collectively identified with a people and who looked outward to other faceless groups with similar representation.

President Nixon, with his bold new diplomacy, changed this "Us-Them-Always-Been" stereotypic leadership concept of world politics which has been in vogue for over three hundred years, and converted it to an "I-Thou-Here-and-Now" confrontation. This reduces the problems to a one-to-one situation in which he and other world leaders fairly can take one another's measure. Two individuals relating to one another here and now in any point in time are the essence of growth. The President, himself no stranger to dynamic interaction, learned from these leadership meetings; the growth of the ideas and policies that affect our future becomes the inevitable result.

## Dynamic Diplomacy

I believe the time has come to update President Wilson's admirable "open convenants of peace, openly arrived at," in the light of a president employing personal diplomacy in a way that none of his predecessors thought possible. "Covenants" implies a *fait accompli,* something to be disclosed after the negotiations have been concluded. But this is 1972, not 1918. I submit that the Nixonian policy of "Coming on live," as the media would have it, will succeed because of "open *agendas* for peace, openly arrived at."

Secretary of State William P. Rogers, reacting to a Congressional rebuff of presidential policies in the form of an anti-foreign aid vote, warned: "The United States cannot afford to retreat from the realities of our *interdependence* with the rest of mankind." \* The Secretary was stressing the President's striving for Freedom to Be, for a mandate to interact dynamically with whomever he meets in his global travels. No one realizes more than Richard Nixon that he is not the same man on Tuesday that he was on Monday. His own six crises (28) bear eloquent testimony to this. The man who bitterly assailed the press on the eve of his gubernatorial defeat in California is not the same man who now boldly spanned continents to bargain with the strong from a position of strength in the hope of alleviating the world's political and financial ills.

I have spoken in previous chapters about the Universal Man, using the President as an archetypical example. *I must emphasize that I single out this country's highest officeholder simply because he is the most visible product of this journey from dependence through independence to interdependence.* It is my hope that if the world's most powerful leader, with all his problems and responsibilities, demonstrates that he does not have to be locked into a particular concept or governed by a predetermined agenda, then we too can realize our potential.

\* Emphasis added.

## Applications to Politics

Echoes of the President's policy are clearly being heard from "them." Leaders are emerging who no longer espouse the group philosophy that pits underachieving blocs of people against other groupings which appear, from a distance, to be more effective.

On his first visit to the United States, President Joseph Broz Tito of fiercely independent Yugoslavia reacted strongly to the Nixonian global policies. "At the present time," Tito told a Los Angeles audience, "when the world, becoming interdependent to a degree never before seen, is getting even smaller, no one should be indifferent and adopt a passive attitude toward all that is going on in the world." President Tito had to earn his spurs before being able to journey abroad and make a statement like that. Communist Yugoslavia, constantly threatened physically and economically by the Russian monolith, has managed to keep its identity and still remain a part of eastern European society.

During the Second World War Tito was fighting for survival and was forced into a dependence on whatever outside help he could get from communist Russia, but with victory came an independence that was far from automatic. International communism, once involved in the internal affairs of his country, was loath to relinquish its foothold. After years of bitter struggle during which his personal safety was often in question, Tito achieved an unprecedented independence within the communist bloc that enabled him to gain true interdependence and to respond to an American President's call for a dialogue that would not be frustrated by positions of power but would depend on a strategy of strength.

It is important, I feel, to clearly understand that a willingness to travel to meet foreign leaders and engage in spontaneous dialogue does not indicate that our President is wallowing in weakness. Rather, he is relying on the experience he has assimilated during his own career, coupled with the

*Dynamic Diplomacy*

strength of his office to enable him to move along the polarities without fear of being judged overly permissive in his reactions to other points of view.

"The problem now," President Nixon told novelist Allen Drury in a recent interview, "is the American spirit. This is a crisis of the spirit that we face. The most important thing of all is to restore the American spirit." What the President was really saying is that the pioneer spirit to which he referred represented the ultimate in the *Freedom to Be*.

In the early days of this republic, a man carved a home out of the wilderness and was prepared to trust in his own freedom to express his own creativity and his own needs and aspirations, and yet give credence to his neighbors' needs, though they differed from his own. The pioneer spirit was really a self-actualizing interdependent spirit, and the President, by his example, has helped to encourage four trends that in my opinion are vital to our national and individual growth.

First, we are shifting gradually from the sickness of passivity to a healthy actualizing orientation. As a nation, we are initiating policy and causing other national leaders to react to us. This is very much to the good, because the new Nixon flexibility in negotiation may force the Chinese, Russian, and other world leaders—friend and foe—to abandon hackneyed phrases that describe their positions and use new words to spontaneously communicate new ideas.

Second, as I have mentioned before, there is a trend toward an "I-Thou-Here-and-Now" pattern of leadership implicit in the President's willingness to shelve group hatreds and distrusts and to concentrate on what one leader is saying to another leader today. No longer is our foreign policy locked in on the attitudes of a previous administration or a previous generation toward spheres of influence. I think that we could well take our cue from this global reexamination to

## Applications to Politics

seek fresh approaches to our own relationships to ethnic and religious groups with whom we may have had slight contact in the past.

The third positive growth trend is, I believe, the fact that we are moving from an intrapersonal to an interpersonal orientation in matters of everyday living. This involves a shift from a defensive, self-seeking style of living to a reaching out toward others in order to understand them better as individuals. We are less and less seeking shelter as members of a group and more and more welcoming a free exchange of ideas, mutually arrived at, that will broaden our lives.

Fourth—and this is most important—in both our personal and our national existence, we are changing from intellectual analysis to emotional experience. More and more we, along with the President, are asking, "How do I feel here and now about this situation?" The psychoanalytic method, which emphasizes a painstaking search of the past to explain present-day motivations, is giving ground to an essentially humanistic view of the importance of the present.

Once again the connection between the international scene and the individual suggests itself. If President Nixon had been bound by the past (as were his predecessors), if he had been hemmed in by an intellectualizing approach rather than permitting himself to work on the level of his gut feeling for spontaneous confrontation with heads of other states, it is quite possible that outmoded enmities and suspicions would have prevailed. We could easily have been led into global war because no one had the courage to begin an actualizing journey that might lead all political polarities toward a point where mutual appreciation of differences might have been achieved.

A practical example: Russians, men as well as women, hug one another in greeting, whereas our society tends to confuse emotional with sexual intimacy. Except in moments of great stress—such as when an American male might embrace a long-lost brother or father—we tend to intellectualize our relationships. But why can't presidents and premiers have the flexibility to compromise on this cultural difference when they meet? Why not a handshake then a hug, or a hug then a handshake? This, viewed by both their peoples, would represent a willingness to acknowledge the interdependence of social systems and a need to express that condition in informal, empathic terms. To those who would shudder at such apostasy, remember that it was not very long ago when *anyone,* let alone a president, suggesting a visit to Peking would be considered subversive at best and at worst treasonous. Times are changing, and attitudes constitute the means of change. As we have seen in the case of the war in Viet Nam, the words "defeat" and "victory" mean vastly different things than they did a scant ten years ago.

"Defeat," President Nixon told a University of Nebraska audience not too long ago, "can be an occasion for learning, for weighing the wisdom of our own purposes, examining the strength of our own resources." He was applying to the world scene the lessons learned through his personal struggle toward interdependence and the political defeats we have discussed earlier in these pages. And in so doing, he has given us all food for thought. Interdependence is emerging as a geopolitical reality not because of some abstract philosophical concept, but because *individuals*—you or I or President Nixon or President Tito—can achieve actualization. It so happens that, with sufficient vision, men in high public office can apply these privately learned experiences in a manner beyond the ken of the average man or woman.

"During this final third of the twentieth century," private citizen Richard M. Nixon wrote in the prestigious quarterly *Foreign Affairs,* "the great race will be between man and change: the race to control change, rather than be controlled

## Applications to Politics

by it. In this race we cannot afford to wait for others to act, and then merely react."

Through his practice of Dynamic Diplomacy, President Nixon has fulfilled the people's mandate by moving purposefully along the established polarities to embrace change. World leaders are responding to his interdependence even as, on a more modest but not less important scale, others may react to us in response to our increasing appreciation of our need to experience and express ourselves interdependently.

# Part Five

# CONCLUSION

# 14

## Freedom to Be

Freedom involves choice. The mere fact of being free implies an opportunity to weigh two or more courses and decide which to take. So it is with the title of this book: *Freedom to Be* might as well be called *choosing* to be, because the inner journey toward interdependence involves a constant examination of values that leads to the making of new decisions.

If we learned nothing else from these pages, we most certainly have found out that the inner journey toward interdependence is a continuous one and that the process makes the struggle well worthwhile.

For it is a struggle. I pointed out at the very start that pain is a condition of growth, and I maintain that the ultimate freedom attainable as a result of this growth is worth it. Others would have it differently. B.F. Skinner, the well known behaviorist, says that a recent book of his "is a fetish

## Conclusion

to demonstrate how things go bad when you make a fetish out of individual freedom and dignity." (46) Skinner would have people live lifes of perpetual dependence, responding in a predictable manner to external stimuli like his famous pigeons and rats, never free to make their own mistakes. This, to me, is sheer regression; rather than move backward to a frightened conformity, we must forge ahead and use our dependence to attain an ultimate dignity.

Perhaps one of the most striking manifestations of this necessary journey toward full actualization is found in group therapy.

The group in the therapeutic process is essentially a growth laboratory. Even as the life experience is characterized by a pattern of relationships, so the group is an encapsulation of those relationships. In life we cut loose from some people, meet others, develop new relationships—some close, some superficial. Relationships with people seem to provide us with our most significant experiences. I feel it is important to relate these experiences to the actualization group, the sensitivity group, the group encounter, the group therapy method—all of which are ways of trying to make contact with others.

The very terms used to denote different groups are themselves of considerable interest. The "sensitivity group" is an early example. "Sensitivity" simply means receptiveness, responsiveness. The group provides us with a method of learning to be more receptive and more responsive, to hear and see, to look and listen, to become more aware of what is going on within ourselves as well as inside of others.

The "encounter group" is a more recent innovation. Interestingly enough in our partially "turned off" society, "encounter" has a diametrically opposite meaning to "sensitivity." It means to come against or, more forcefully, to com-

*Freedom to Be*

bat and do battle with. A recent book on encounter therapy has, as its dust-jacket design, two arrows clashing.

Curiously, although these two orientations—sensitivity and encounter—at first glance seem very different, in reality they are most compatible; they are polarities toward which we must strive, like the love-anger and strength-weakness polarities discussed in detail in Chapter 2. Life requires that ultimately we learn to tune into others while at the same time standing up to them, much as the characters created by John Bunyan in *Pilgrim's Progress* (6) had to do.

There are many similarities between the modern group and the traditional family unit. I like to think of the group as the therapeutic family or the "second-chance family." Historically, the American family has gone through three stages. The first stage I refer to as grandparent-centered stage. The nuclei of this family are the grandparents. Just outside this center are the parents; finally, on the periphery, are the children. The grandparent, of course, is king, and parents and children must defer to the aged. The two younger generations have certain obligations toward and dependencies on the grandparents, who are considered the wise ones and are looked to for guidance.

During the past twenty or thirty years, most American families have belonged to my second category, the parent-centered unit. In my own case, my father was raised in Sweden in a family with ties to Prussian tradition. The parent was the center of the family, the children were next, and the grandparents were the outermost group. The emphasis was on pleasing the producers—that is, the mother and father. Their reputation was most important and a united front had to be shown to the outside world.

Currently we have the third family category, which can be called the child-centered family. The grandparents are com-

## Conclusion

pletely outside the main group, often physically absent. The parents occupy the second level, and the child is the nucleus. Partly as the result of the popularity of "child psychology," child-centered families have been much in vogue. Instead of pleasing the wise grandparents or the productive parents, the family tries to please the young—to please the consumers, if you will.

What has all this to do with actualization? Consider the group as a *therapeutic family*. One of the requirements for group participation is that each person take responsibility for himself. This taking of responsibility leads to an actualizing orientation and makes it possible to understand the progression from dependence through independence to interdependence. In the group, the emotionally dependent people do not control the others, as happens in the child-centered family.

The dynamics of what I call the topdog-underdog pattern of relationships become readily apparent in the group, making it possible for them to be changed. No longer is the topdog in charge, no longer is the underdog indirectly controlling; each one has to find his own way by his own method, to locate the route he will take to find the ultimate Freedom to Be.

The poet and philosopher Kahlil Gibran (13) describes the ultimate state of interdependence with uncommon sensitivity. Two truly interdependent people, he writes, are like two pillars of a temple that are joined together at the top but still remain individual, like the oak tree and the cypress that grow not in each other's shadow, like the strings of a lute that quiver with the same music but still sing alone.

Gibran has another thought which I believe to be especially pertinent: "Let me not be too proud of my safety. Even as a Thief in the jail is safe from another thief." This statement gets at the central idea of this book, for the actualizing person, in a group or alone, must take the risk of not being safe. If we wish, we can stay in "jail" and let B.F. Skinner see to our needs; or we can be truly free and choose to take the risk of communicating and dealing with one another in order to experience actualization. This is the challenge of Freedom to Be; it provides us with an opportunity to get out of our own personal jail and to change our orientation toward others as well as toward ourselves.

The actualizing person needs to develop both strength and weakness, anger and love. Werner von Braun, who made the move from Peenemunde to Houston in one graceful, ideological bound, is an interesting example of successful self-actualization with particular reference to the love-anger, strength-weakness polarities. Here he is described by writer Norman Mailer (20) in *Life* magazine:

> Since he had, in contrast to his delivery, a big, burly squared-off bulk of a body, which gave hint of the ponderous deliberation, the methodical ruthlessness of more than one Russian bureaucrat, Von Braun's relatively small voice, darting eyes and semaphoric presentations of lip made it obvious that he was a man of opposites. He revealed a confusing aura of strength and vulnerability, of calm and agitation, cruelty and concern, phlegm and sensitivity, which would have given fine play to the talents of so virtuoso an actor as Mr. Rod Steiger. Von Braun had, in fact, something of Steiger's soft voice, that play of force and weakness which speaks of consecration and vanity, dedication and indulgence, steel and fat.

Such a delicate play of opposites can result from the symphony of the group process. The group provides an opportunity to enter into contact with other human beings, to do battle, to love and hurt with other human beings, to feel

## Conclusion

with each other, and so to develop the family of man in which each of us stands alone and yet is interdependently *response-able*.

My four freedoms are the freedom to be interdependent, the freedom not to be dependent except in the context of that interdependence, the freedom to know the difference, and the freedom to choose.

A magazine writer once asked me what would happen if a married couple seeking self-actualization at the Institute grew at different rates so that the marriage was jeopardized because of the uneven growth. After first explaining that we put estranged married couples in different groups but encouraged them to "date" socially away from the groups, I replied: "I think the assumption that you shouldn't have therapy because it is going to cause some pain is probably right—concerning the pain. But I think it is based on a philosophy which denies the importance of the polarities of one's existence. My philosophy of therapy is that you cannot live or be alive without pain and suffering, and every polar feeling has its own kind of pain as well as joy."

When a person suggests that he or she is ready for graduation from a group (a request that most often must be made several times over an extended period), we like to ask: "You've learned to talk the talk. Are you ready to walk the walk?"—that is, the walk toward self-actualizing either with your present partner or alone in a spirit of true interdependence. Quite often we have found that, when members of a group first suggest graduation, they are not yet ready to begin "walking happy," as the title song of a Broadway musical had it a couple of years ago. As I've pointed out at some length in Chapter 9, divorce and the resulting trial and error implicit in the seeking of a new relationship may be the path toward achieving the interdependence that will satisfy a self-actualizing person.

*Freedom to Be*

An actualizing person is one who sees his life in perspective and who is willing to risk the dissolution of old relationships in a search for a better future. Remember that most so-called independence—whether it be that of a teenager doing his own thing or that of a marriage partner demanding her rights—is really counter-dependent; it is an independence *against* or *freedom from* something rather than a *freedom to be* with assurance that enables its possessor to interact freely with other people.

Self-actualization requires an acceptance of *response–ability*. President Harry Truman's famous desk sign "The buck stops here" admirably sums up the need for a man in a position of responsibility to be able to accept that responsibility. There was no one to whom President Truman could pass the buck.

Whether it be for the President of the United States or for you and I, actualization as I envision it is a positive attitude and its end, interdependence, is a "now" concept. What is happening, here and now, between this nation and that, between this man and this woman, is what concerns us in our never-ending journey toward an actualizing life. Although I would not go as far as the late Henry Ford and say that "History is bunk," I will say that personal history in the form of Freudian analysis deals too much in what has happened and not enough in the here-and-now. *Actualization Therapy* stresses instead, taking *response–ability*—the personal ability to respond in the now.

I have used famous people such as President Nixon and Doctor von Braun as examples in order to clearly point the way to our own potential. The theories set down between these pages already are winning recognition. For example, Dr. Laura J. Singer-Magdoff, on the faculty of the American Institute for Psychotherapy and Psychoanalysis and a recognized expert in the field of interpersonal relationships, notes that "Within marriage—the most intimate and personal of

*Conclusion*

all relationships—we must be ourselves. We must train ourselves to open up, to communicate directly with our spouses, to remove the mask of independence." (45)

This growth toward interdependence, within marriage or without, is not a journey whose destination is an emotional pot of gold at the end of the rainbow. It is rather a neverending process of experiencing and expressing our *total* selves. It is a trip to be continuously enjoyed, a key which each of us may have for the risking. This idea is beautifully expressed in this verse by Dr. Shirley Kashoff:

### THE KEY TO FREEDOM

>I used to think that Freedom
>Was what someone gave to me.
>Until I found that I was bound
>By nameless heavy chains
>I could not see.
>
>I used to think that Freedom
>Was what someone gave to me.
>Until I learned that what I'd earned
>Was simply my permission
>To use that very freedom
>That no one but myself
>Could give to me.
>
>Those locks and bonds and prisons
>Are the things we've learned to hate
>Yet these most despised constructions
>Are identically the ones
>We have masterfully come to create.
>
>I've spent my lifetime waiting
>For someone to set me free.
>I could not grow
>I didn't know
>That in my very hands I held
>The key.

# Bibliography

1. Albee, George. "The Short, Unhappy Life of Clinical Psychology," *Psychology Today,* Sept. 1970 B, pp. 42–43, 71.
2. Albee, George. "The Uncertain Future of Clinical Psychology," *American Psychologist,* 25, 2. Dec. 1970 A, pp. 1071–1080.
3. Bennis, Warren G. "Organic Populism," *Psychology Today,* Feb. 1970, pp. 48–71.
4. Bleuler, Eugen, in Brown, J.F. *Psychodynamics of Abnormal Behavior,* New York: McGraw-Hill, 1940.
5. Brammer, Lawrence M., and Shostrom, Everett L. *Therapeutic Psychology,* Englewood Cliffs, New Jersey: Prentice-Hall, 1960.
6. Bunyan, John. *Pilgrim's Progress,* New York: Holt, Rinehart and Winston, Paper.
7. Burke, Louis H., and Shostrom, Everett L. *With This Ring,* New York: McGraw-Hill Book Company, 1958.
8. *Diagnostic and Statistical Manual of Mental Disorders,* Washington, D.C.: American Psychiatric Association, 1952.
9. Dunnam, Maxie D., Herbertson, Gary J., and Shostrom, Everett L. *The Manipulator and the Church,* New York: Abingdon Press, 1968.
10. Erikson, Erik. *Childhood and Society,* New York: Norton, 1950.
11. Frankl, Viktor E. *Man's Search for Meaning,* New York: Beacon Press, 1963.
12. Gibran, Kahlil. *The Madman,* New York: Knopf, 1918.

*Bibliography*

13. Gibran, Kahlil. *The Prophet,* New York: Knopf, 1923.
14. Graves, Ralph. *Life,* Vol. 72, No. 15, April 21, 1972, p. 3.
15. Lao Tse. *The Way of Life,* New York: Mentor Books, 1955.
16. Lawrence, D.H. *Apocalypse,* New York: Viking, 1966.
17. Leary, Timothy. *Interpersonal Diagnosis of Personality,* New York: Ronald, 1957.
18. Lodge, Henry Cabot. *The New York Times,* January 2, 1972.
19. Lowen, Alexander. *The Betrayal of the Body,* New York: Macmillan, 1966.
20. Mailer, Norman. "A Fire on The Man," *Life,* August 29, 1969, p. 33.
21. Maslow, Abraham H. *The Farther Reaches of Human Nature,* New York: Viking, 1971.
22. Maslow, Abraham H. *Motivation and Personality,* New York: Harper and Row, 1954.
23. Maslow, Abraham H. *Toward a Psychology of Being,* Princeton, New Jersey: D. Van Nostrand Co., 1962.
24. May, Rollo. *Existence,* New York: Basic Books, 1958.
25. May, Rollo. *Love and Will,* New York: W.W. Norton, 1969.
26. May, Rollo. *Psychology and the Human Dilemma,* Princeton, New Jersey: D. Van Nostrand Co., 1967.
27. Murphy, Gardner. *Human Potentialities,* New York: Basic Books, 1958.
28. Nixon, Richard. *Six Crises,* New York: Doubleday, 1962.
29. Nixon, Richard. Quotation to Premier Chou of China, *Los Angeles Times,* p. 10, part 1, Feb. 26, 1972.
30. Otto, Herbert. *Group Methods to Actualize Human Potential,* Beverly Hills, California: Holistic Press, 1970.
31. Pascal, Blaise, Penses #277, *Provincial Letters,* New York: Modern Library, 1941, p. 92.
32. Perls, Frederick, et al. *Gestalt Therapy,* New York: Julian Press, 1951.
33. Perls, Frederick. *Gestalt Therapy Verbatim,* Lafayette, California: Real People Press, 1969.

34. Pesso, Albert. *Movement in Psychotherapy*, New York: New York University Press, 1969.
35. Rogers, Carl R. *Client-Centered Therapy*, Boston: Houghton Mifflin Company, 1959.
36. Rogers, Carl R. *On Becoming a Person*, Boston: Houghton Mifflin Company, 1961.
37. Russell, Bertrand. *Portraits From Memory*, New York: Simon and Shuster, 1963.
38. Shapiro, David. *Neurotic Styles*, New York: Basic Books, 1965.
39. Shostrom, Everett L., and Kavanaugh, James. *Between Man and Woman*, Los Angeles: Nash, 1971.
40. Shostrom, Everett L. *Man, the Manipulator*, New York: Abingdon Press, 1967.
41. Shostrom, Everett L. *Manual for the Personal Orientation Inventory*, San Diego, California: Educational and Industrial Testing Service, 1962.
42. Shostrom, Everett L. *Manual for the Caring Relationship Inventory*, San Diego, California: Educational and Industrial Testing Service, 1965.
43. Shostrom, Everett L., and Brammer, L.M. *The Dynamics of the Counseling Process*, New York: McGraw-Hill Book Company, 1952.
44. Sidey, Hugh. "The Economic Bombshell," *Life*, August 27, 1971, pp. 20–21.
45. Singer-Magdoff, Laura J. Quotation, *National Enquirer*, Nov. 14, 1971.
46. Skinner, B.F. *Beyond Freedom and Dignity*, New York: Alfred A. Knopf, 1971.
47. Stuart, Grace. *Narcissus*, London: George Allen and Unwin Limited, 1956.
48. Tillich, P. *The Courage to Be*, New Haven: Yale University Press, 1952.
49. Toffler, Alvin. *Future Shock*, New York: Bantam, 1971.
50. Victoroff, Victor. "The Assumptions We Live By." *Etc.* XVI, 1958, pp. 17–18.

## Bibliography

51. Watts, Alan W. *The Book: On the Taboo Against Knowing Who You Are*, New York: Collier, 1966.
52. Watts, Alan W. *The Wisdom of Insecurity*, New York: Pantheon Books, 1949.

# Index

abnormality, 55, 61
actualization, 55; group, 176; meaning of, 71
actualized, self-concept, 124
actualizing, 155; as a concept and process, 74; behavior, 62; frame of reference, 62; person, 84, 154, 159, 181; relationship, 159
agape, 104–5, 109, 159
agape stage, 108
Albee, George, 53, 55
alienation, 133
American family unit, 177
amoeba, 76
anger, 69, 76; demands, 29; dimension, expressing of physically, 77; expressions, 29; fear of behavioral expression, 69
"Anger-Love," basic polarity, 28, 58, 65, 68
annoyance, 69
anxiety, 76
*Apocalypse*, 41
appreciation of differences, 160
Aquarius, age of, 116
assertion, 48
assumptions, questioning our, 89
attacking and blaming, 58
Australia, 148
authentic love, 104, 110
avoidance, 61
avoiding, 34, 61

Barron, Frank, 11
basic polarities, 70
behavioral expression of anger, 67

Bennis, Warren, 42
*Betrayal of the Body*, 80
Bioenergetic Analysis, 84
Bishop, George, 5
black-and-white game, 72
blaming, 33; and attacking, 58
"blessed trinity," 156
Bleuler, Eugen, 12
body trip, 83
Britain, 143
British Empire, 142
Buber, Martin, 106
Buhler, Charlotte, 123
"bully," 33
Bunyan, John, 177

"calculator," 34
Capacity for Aggression, 56; for Intimate Contact, 56
capitalism, 98
caring, 47, 48
Caring Relationship Inventory, 103
caring sequence, 107
Castro, Fidel, 145
Chamberlain, Neville, 160
Chaplin, Charlie, 68
"charity," 105
child-centered family, 177
China, 147, 161
Chinese, 163
choosing to be, 175
Chou, Premier of China, 10
Christian tradition, 86
"clinging vine," 34
Coffey, Hubert, 11

# Index

communism, 98
compassion, 47, 48
conniving and controlling, 58, 60
contact vs. withdrawal, 76
continuum, 65
control, 82
controlling and conniving, 58, 60
cope-ability, 121
counter-dependence, 85; vs. independence, 181
countervaluing, 158
courage, 47, 48
*Courage to Be,* 130
Cox, Wally, 45
creative consciousness, 52; process, four stages, 127

Davis, Sammy, 9
"dead center," 65
Declaration of Independence, 113; Marital Independence, 114
dependence, 17, 74; stage, 156
dependency, 27
depression, 49
Diagnostic and Statistical Manual of Mental Disorders, 59; diagnostic efforts, 53
"dictator," 34
"directional tendency," 123
divorce, 115; Divorce-Lib, 114, 116 ff.; Divorce-Lib movement, 120
dropout movement, 85
drug scene, 85
Drury, Allen, 169
Dynamic Diplomacy, 164 ff., 172

ecology, 17, 71
education, 85
Eisenhower, 153
Emerson, Ralph Waldo, 139
"emotional education," 85
emotions, 76
empathy, 104 f., 159; stage, 107
encounter approach, 150

Erikson, Erick, 53
eros, 104, 159; stage, 107, 109
excitement, 83
existential movement, 129
existentialist, 129
expanding of emotional expression, 65
expectations, high, 91
expression, 150
eye specialist analogy, 72

"facial touch," 78
"family argument," 77
fear, 52, 76; of anger, 67; of moving forward, 52; of paranoia, 159
fears, high, 91
feel, 52
feeling of cutting off, 82; feeling-oriented vs. head-oriented, 84; "maxi-swing," 65
feelings, 67, 83; mild or timorous, 67; "mini-swings," 67
"feels," 50
"fertile voids," 43
four freedoms, 48, 180; four polarities, 48
Frankl, Viktor, 5, 72, 131
freedom, 129, 175; *Freedom, The Key to* (poem), 182 f., *Freedom to Be,* 53 ff., 84, 86, 121, 175
Freud, Sigmund, 52, 129, 134
Freudian analysis, 181; psychoanalysis, 21
friendship, 104 f., 105, 109, 159; stage, 108
Fromm, Erich, 108, 133
"full feeling repertoire," 67
functional vs. malfunctional theories, 61
*Future Shock,* 115

Gestalt therapy, 130 f.; *Gestalt Therapy Verbatim,* 144
Gibran, Kahlil, 178

# Index

God, 86
grace, 71, 86 f.
Graves, Ralph, 68
"grounding," 82
group encounter, 176; group therapy, 176; group session, 93
"groupitis," 163 f.
"growing edges," 71; growing person, 38
growth, 29; alternative, 39; -orientation, 28, 39, 48; -oriented, 27; -oriented person, 27, 123
guilt, 120

Harlow, Harry, 108
hatred, 69
have, 52; "have to," 50 f.
"head-oriented," 67, 84; vs. feeling-oriented, 84
Hemingway, Ernest, 42
Hepburn, Katherine, 67
Hitler, Adolph, 45, 59, 160
homeostatic balance, 70
homicide, 59
hostility, 59, 69, 150
human encounter, 103, 107; defined as love, 103; four stages of, 110
human heart, rhythm, 74
*Humanistic Psychology*, 150
*Humanistic Revolution* film, 124
"humanistic view," of therapy, 38
Huxley, Aldous, 42

"I-Thou-Here-and-Now," concept of, 167; pattern of leadership, 170
"I-Thou" relationship, 106
independence, 20, 27, 42, 74; vs. counter-dependence, 181
inner balance, 71
"Inner Supreme Court," 12
Institute of Therapeutic Psychology, 5

"intentionality," 154
interchange, expressive vs. repressive, 149
interdependence, 16, 22 ff., 42, 55, 74, 98, 172, 181 f.; of social systems, 171
interdependent stage, 91, 156
interpersonal orientation vs. intrapersonal, 170

Jefferson, 126
jockstrap complex, 90
Joleen, 94, 106; and Lou, 17, 22, 35, 49, 89, 91 ff., 103, 106, 110, 159
Jonah Complex, 158
"joy," 78
"judge," 33
Jung, 134

Kashoff, Dr. Shirley, 182
Kennedy, John F., 28, 166
Khrushchev, 45
Knotts, Don, 45

Lao-Tze, 12, 72
latitude, 72
Lawrence, D. H., 41
Leary, Timothy, 35
Lincoln, 126
"loaded with love," 45
Lodge, Henry Cabot, 60
logotherapy, 73
Lou, and Joleen, 17, 22, 35, 49, 89, 91 ff., 103, 110, 159
love, 89, 103 f., 119; "Love-Anger," basic polarity, 28, 58, 65, 68; as human encounter, 103; demands, 29; dimension, 69, 78, 104; dimension, expressing of physically, 78; expressions, 29
loving life, 130
Lowen, Alexander, 75, 80, 83, 86;

# Index

Lowen and Bioenergetic Therapy film, 75
Magnificent Men, 123; characteristics of, 135
Mailer, Norman, 179
malfunctional theories vs. functional theories, 61
*Man, the Manipulator*, 20, 106, 154
manipulation, 58, 71, 107, 155
manipulative behavior, 55; marriage, 92; processes, 31; response forms, 31; role, 131; ways of behaving, 71
*Man's Search for Meaning*, 72
Mao, Chairman, 147
Marital Independence, Declaration of, 114
marriage, 109, 119; as a workshop for growth, 103; excision of, 120; journey, 92; structure of actualizing, 118
Maslow, Abraham, 5, 27, 55 f., 74, 104, 123, 125, 158
masochistic behavior, 58
May, Rollo, 5, 51, 105, 129, 154
"maxi-swing" feeling, 65
means vs. ends, 73
mental illness, 52
military containment game, 149
"mini-swings" feelings, 67
modulation of affect, 67, 70
moment, learning to live in, 73
Murphy, Gardner, 5, 127
"must," 50 ff.

nadir or "valley" experiences, 42
narcissistic behavior, 60
*Narcissus*, 69
nations, from persons to, 139
needs to actualize or grow, 62; need to survive, 62
negative reinforcement, 62
neuroses, defined, 52

"nice-guy," 31
Nixon-Chou, 149
Nixon, President Richard M., 5, 27, 61, 149, 154, 161, 164 ff., 169, 171 f.
"no," 77
nonactualizing person, defined, 154
"normal" neurotic behavior, 55
normality, 61
nucleus, characteristic of actualizing, 155

"object," 49; object-self, 50
"objective" vs. "subjective" orientation, 49
"Olympic Gold Medal Winners," 123
Otto, Herbert, 68
"oughts," 74

paradox of change, 9
paranoid psychosis, 59
Parker, Dorothy, 67
Pascal, Blaise, 12
Peking, 171
Perls, Frederick S., 5, 16, 104, 130, 144
Personal Orientation Inventory, 56
persons, from nations to, 139
Pesso, Albert, 35
philia, 105
*Pilgrim's Progress*, 177
pleasing and placating, 58
pleasure, 80 f.; *Pleasure*, 81; contrasted with power, 84; "pleasure formula," 86
POI, 56
polarities, 53, 65
polarity: "Anger-Love," 28, 58, 65, 68; "Strength-Weakness," 28, 58, 65, 67, 79
politics, applications to, 137
*Portraits from Memory*, 21
positive reinforcement, 62

## Index

prescriptions, 53
present, living in the, 73
"protector," 31
psychiatry, 38, 55
psychoanalytic method, 170
psychodiagnosis, 53
psychologist, 104; therapeutic, 104
psychoanalysis, Freudian, 21
psychopathic, 60
psychopathology, 61
psychotherapist, 132
psychotherapy, 71
psychotic behavior, 55; depression, 59
Puritan tradition, 86
pursuit of happiness, 131

Reichians, 87
resentment, 69
response-ability, 180 f.
responsibility, 49, 51, 53, 129
rhythm, 71; human heart, 74; of life, 72; of living, 65
right and wrong concern, 72
risk, 65
Rogers, Carl, 5, 128
Rogers, Jimmy, 9
Rogers, William P., 167
role-reversal, 96 f.
romantic love, 109
Roosevelt, Eleanor, 42, 109
Roosevelt, Franklin D., 121, 153
Rusk, Dean, 93
Russell, Bertrand, 21
Russia, 97
Russians, 163

sadistic behavior, 59
Saint-Exupéry, Antoine de, 89, 98
Satir, Virginia, 5, 75
schizoid tendency, 61
schizophrenia, 61, 70
Schweitzer, Albert, 109

self-actualization, 42, 71 ff., 181; as a process, 74; defined, 74
self-actualizing, 124
self-control, 42
self-regard, 56
self-worth, 56
sense of responsibility, 60
sensitive clinician vs. hard-headed scientist, 129
"Sensitivity," 176; group, 176
serial or temporary marriage, 115
Shapiro, David, 53
"should," 50; "shoulds," 74
"sickness view," of mental illness, 52
Sidey, Hugh, 165
Sinatra, Frank, 9
Singer-Magdoff, Dr. Laura J., 181
Skinner, B. F., 62, 175
Smith, Sydney, 119
social systems, interdependence of, 171
sociopath, 60
sociopathic exploitation, 60
South Africa, Union of, 146
Soviet Union, 96, 140
Stalin, Joseph, 45
Steiger, Rod, 179
stereotypic control, 164
Stevenson, Adlai, 153
strength, basic polarity, 60; bombardment, 68; demands, 30; expressions, 30
"Strength-Weakness," basic polarity, 28, 58, 65, 67, 79
Stuart, Grace, 69
stuck on strength, 45
subject, 48, 50
Subjective Stance, 48; view, 49
suicide, 59
survival, 29; -orientation, 28, 39
taboo on admitting weakness, 68
taboo on tenderness, 70

191

## Index

Taoism, 126
tenderness, 69
Tertium Quid, 143, 149; Formuli, 43
*The Book on Taboo Against Knowing Who We Are*, 72
therapeutic family, as a group, 178; therapeutic psychologist, 104
Tillich, Paul, 5, 130
Tito, President Joseph Broz, 168
Toffler, Alvin, 115
*total* being of self, experiencing and expressing, 182
*Toward a Psychology of Being*, 27
"trial marriage," 115
"trip," taking a, 155
triton ti, 43
Truman, Harry, 61, 181

"unconscious," 132, 134
unconscious, defined, 132
U. N. (United Nations), 60, 163
United States, 96
United States International University, 22
Universal Man, 153, 155; stages of, 156

"Us-Them-Always-Been," concept of, 167

Victoroff, Victor M., 90
Viet Nam, 171; North and South, 149
von Braun, Dr. Werner, 179, 181
vulnerability, 68

wallow in weakness, 45
want, 50, 52
"wants," 50
Watts, Alan, 5, 72 f., 132
"weakling," 34
weakness, 60, 68; demands, 30; expressions, 30, 80; feelings of, 68
"Weakness-Strength," basic polarity, 28, 58, 65, 67, 79
Wertheimer, Max, 126
Willkie, Wendell, 139
Wilson, President, 167
winning-losing concept, 166
withdrawal vs. contact, 76
withdrawing, 61; and avoiding, 58
Women's Liberation Movement, 106